PROMISE
OF THE
ROAD

Based on a True Story

by
Jacklyn Landis

GoMyStory.com
3070 Collins Court
The Villages, FL 32163
757-439-7700
www.GoMyStory.com

Cover design: fromfrank.com / Kate Smith

Page design & typography: GoMyStory.com /John W Prince

Printed in the United States of America

Library of Congress Control Number: 2018953441

Landis, Jacklyn

Promise of the Road

The historical fictionalization of the difficult journey of the close-knit, loving Sampley family from the Texas Dustbowl across America to California during the Great Depression.

ISBN-10: 1986796752   ISBN-13: 978-1986796750

Acknowledgments

I can never adequately thank my husband, Jerry Landis, who believed in me and genuinely felt that this story needed to be told.

I am thankful to the Sampley family for the many ways they shared their life with me, and the positive influence that made in my life.

A very special thanks to cover designer, Kate Smith.

My gratitude goes out to the Sampley Family and to my Son, Daughter, and Grandchildren for their encouragement and feedback on readings.

Jacklyn Landis

It was an enormously hard life...
But there was also a sense of great
satisfaction in being a child with
valuable work to do and, being able
to do it well, to function in this world.

Margot Hentoff
The Forgotten Children

Chapter One

On a summer day in the year 1931, the rising sun flooded the sod bank house with diluted sunshine. A hint of the blistering heat to come. The Sampley homestead, an unobtrusive dot on the Texas Panhandle, was awakening to a new day. Pauline, careful not to rouse older sister June, slowly rolled off their shared mat. She lay still, letting her body drink in the coolness of the packed dirt floor. Brothers, Delbert and Dale, lying back to back stirred and then breathed easy.

Pauline peered around the sod block wall. Her sleepy green eyes searched for Mama and Daddy in the dark, musty room. Stacked crates embraced their neatly folded clothes. Their bed was empty. Covers made up.

Thin and small for her age, Pauline hurried across the threshold and up the carved out earthen steps of the sunken soddy. Bony knees tucked under her chin, she waited atop the grass-covered roof. Her bare feet swayed to and fro across dry prickly stems. She turned toward the familiar sound of rustling corn and knew Daddy was cleaning his moonshine still in preparation for night. The slamming of the hen house door was the signal that the last batch of corn liquor was now safely hidden under the straw.

Pauline remembered early spring. Daddy said, "You kids unhitch Nellie and ol' Dan from the plow." When they finished, they joined Daddy at the edge of the freshly plowed field. Daddy stretched out the palm of his hand revealing a single kennel of golden corn and a small broken twig. He spoke in a deep monotone voice, eyes rotating from one child to the next, "Push one o' these seeds into the top of each row—stop when you reach the first crease on your pointer finger. Carefully brush the soil back into the hole. Then measure the distance on your stick and do it again as you move on down the row."

Deliberately, one foot in front of the other, Pauline listened as she walked the row opposite Daddy.

"Pauline, this 'ere seed corn is gonna keep the inside of these pockets from lookin' like Hoover flags," Daddy snickered while slowly shaking his head from side to side. "Yep, Pauline, anyone voting fer Hoover in this 'ere election comin' up deserves to see his empty pockets a-flappin' in the breeze. This corn is our insurance. Whichever way the election goes, we Sampleys will have some earnin's a-comin' in."

Later, as they walked into the soddy, Pauline shook her head in agreement with Daddy—just like always. She thought silently that even Mama had to admit the money from picking cotton alone was not enough to make ends meet. Mama had explained, more often than Pauline wanted to think about, that selling corn liquor to city folks was the only means Daddy had to keep his family from going hungry.

Just the thought of Daddy's forbidden moonshine business brought about daydreams of Mama standing in the window of the soddy, wringing her hands at the sight of an approaching car followed by a streak of dust—the Feds in search of the prohibited corn liquor.

Mama and Daddy were walking toward her now, their smiling eyes beaming at their girl.

Daddy hollered, "Pauline, wake the others, the cotton fields are awaitin'."

As Pauline dressed for work, she criticized her reflection in a piece of broken mirror. Her new bonnet framed her pale freckled skin and forced her bobbed, carrot-red bangs down over her eyebrows. Stretching her neck, she tugged at the already uncomfortable tie of her shawl. She remembered the night before and the consistent rhythm of Mama's treadle sewing machine, her child-size foot rocking back and forth on the ornate, iron foot pedal that had nearly lulled Pauline to sleep. Then, finally, the hush as she finished.

Mama had turned toward Pauline, holding a shawl in one hand and a slat bonnet, crown stiff with cardboard, in the other.

Pauline nervously awaited the well-deserved tongue-lashing that was sure to come.

"Now young lady, I want to see you wear this all day tomorrow or you'll blister for sure. And if the sun doesn't blister you, I will!" Memories of Mama rubbing Pauline's hot, red skin with smelly vinegar made her shiver. "Now, don't be leaving these lay someplace, the cloth is expensive." Her voice had trailed off as if she was already thinking of something else.

Gratefully, the guilt Pauline felt about losing her other hat and shawl had begun to fade. She remembered the words she had heard Daddy say so often, *"Tomorrow's another day, Pauline. Tomorrow's another day."*

* * * * *

Eight-year-old Pauline sat in the spacious back seat of the family's 1920 Oakland. She squinted through a pinhole made by linking her thumb and index finger together, as Daddy did when he tried to read prices at the grocery store. She searched her familiar, predictable world, examining the silhouette of Uncle Charlie and Aunt Julia's house off in the distance. They had the luxury of a windmill, but their above ground Sears and Roebuck house was hot and stuffy in the summertime, and cold in winter.

As Pauline waited, she repeatedly flipped a piece of torn upholstery back and forth. Puffs of lint and dust floated across streaks of sunlight. Her attention shifted to Nellie and Ol' Dan swaggering toward a shady spot close to the barn.

Delbert, the elder of her two brothers, but short for his age, strutted toward the car. His complexion, red as usual, looked as if he were mad about something. Dale, the youngest, annoyed him by kicking dirt at his heels. June, crumpled hair-ribbon dangling from her fingertips, walked slightly behind Mama, slouching to show her displeasure at being hurried. Last was precious Daddy, tall, lean, and hollow-cheeked.

Pauline's voice was garbled by the tires bumping over potholes in the dirt road. "Maaaaa, Maaaaa, will you bake us some cookkiiees when we get hoommee?"

"I suppose," she said with a tenderhearted smile that was all hers. "But you children will have to take Delbert's old wagon out and pick me up some cow chips to burn in the wood stove."

All the children, except Delbert, jumped up and down on the seat allowing the roughness of the road to distort their high-pitched squeals. Pauline wondered if Delbert was too old for such shenanigans.

Nearing the cotton fields, Pauline could see families of farm workers standing in line. She knew they were waiting for their shoulder bags, which would be filled with cotton over and over again throughout the day.

The car had barely rolled to a stop when the back doors flung open. The four Sampley children, even Delbert, all hurried to the shady side of the check-in-station where a group of children had gathered.

A tall girl with stringy hair swaggered toward Pauline. "How much cotton ya think yer gonna pick, freckles?"

Pauline felt a warm flush sweeping over her as she sucked in a deep breath. After June protectively edged closer, Pauline squeezed her eyes shut tight and stuck her tongue out real hard. Then, she proudly turned on her heels and strolled toward Daddy who was busy talking with a small group of men near the counter.

Pauline cradled Daddy's right leg with both arms. She swayed from side to side, stiff-legged, her weight coming down one foot at a time, causing Daddy to brace himself. Half-heartedly she listened as the men talked.

"What we're gettin' paid fer pickin' this 'ere cotton ain't enough to even buy shoes fer the youngins. I hear tell that some folks has been forced to go—ah–bootleggin' jest to put bread on the table."

Pauline gasped aloud while quickly looking up into the faces of the men. *If Mama had said it once, she had said it a thousand times, "The Prohibition Act was enacted in 1919."*

Mama and Daddy had forbidden any of the Sampley children to speak of moonshine to anyone outside the family. A hush fell over the group until someone spoke, changing the subject.

"Yep, ya'd sure think ol' President Hoover would find a quicker way to execute us than starve us to death. I jest hope to God that someday he hears his backbone scratchin' his stomach from emptiness," said a man with a ruddy complexion and sagging face.

Suddenly, Daddy straightened up, nearly knocking Pauline off her feet. He took hold of her hand, shaking his head hopelessly as they walked away from the group. "Trouble is—we got us a President who has no solutions to the problems and ain't likely to ever come up with any. Come on Pauline, let's get this Sampley clan to work before Ol' Man Sun gets overhead."

Pauline gazed out over the never-ending rows of cotton, dreading the sharp, flesh-tearing branches that could only be soothed by warm salt water and horse liniment.

* * * * *

On the way home the four Sampley children leaned out the windows of the Oakland. The wind soothed their warm faces and dried their sweat soaked hair. The sight of the soddy gave Pauline a surge of energy. The family filed out of the car heading for the windmill where a long-handled dipper hung from a wire attached to one of the legs of the tower. Coming from deep underground— the water in the well house was ice cold. The family savored every drop as if it was Holy Communion.

Pauline and Dale rambled off across the desert, towing Delbert's rusty, red wagon in search of cow chips, prairie coal, as Daddy called it. Their shrill giggles and squeals of success echoed against the stark silence of the land.

* * * * *

Throughout the stifling days of summer, they walked the cotton rows. Mama attempted to help pass the time by quizzing her children on the alphabet, spelling, and arithmetic. That was the summer Pauline tried to convince Mama that she had a hearing problem!

She could see Mama about two rows over, amongst the gray-green leaves and white puffs of cotton. She saw just the top of her head, her bent shoulders, and perspiration-stained collar. Mama was teaching again. Pauline thought it embarrassing when others overheard and curiously glanced their way. Mama seemed not to notice and simply continued quizzing her children. Pauline could hear the growing fatigue in her Mama's voice, but knew perfectly well she would not let that stand in the way of her mission.

"Delbert, four times four?"

"Sixteen, Mama."

"June, spell 'arithmetic.'"

"a- r- i -t- h- m- e- t- i- c."

"Dale, five plus one?"

"Six, Mama."

"Pauline, spell 'home.'"

"Huh?"

Pauline felt guilty. *"I can't help it if the sun is hot and I'm sweating. Why do I have to learn all this dumb stuff anyway? Mama is being too hard on us."* She listened as Mama started around the group again.

"Delbert, spell 'automobile.'"

"June, what's nine times nine?"

"Dale, ten minus seven is?"

Pauline kept her head down and worked faster than usual, secretly encouraged by Mama's previous acceptance of her newfound hearing impairment.

"Pauline, spell 'lazy.'"

"Huh?"

"Pauline, are you ready for lunch?"

"Yes!" She replied as she struggled to pull the heavy, cotton-filled bag off of her shoulder.

Suddenly Daddy was on his haunches in front of her, looking hard into her eyes as if she were hollow.

His words stung as he spoke, "Pauline," he said in a loud whisper. "Look at your Mama! See her sweat-soaked hair clinging to the back of her neck? Her back must be achin' 'bout now, don't cha think?"

Pauline's brows knitted together as she briefly cut her eyes in Mama's direction. Then stared back at the hurt expression in Daddy's eyes, an expression she never wanted to see again. Hot tears flowed freely across her crimson cheeks. She reached out— arms open wide, hiding her wet face in the crevice of Daddy's neck. Then she felt his arms around her, open palms and fingertips resting firmly on her shoulder blades. Pauline strained to hear his barely audible words.

"You know you need to talk to your Mama now, don't you?

Chapter Two

Daddy's parched lips blew in and out through the small metal slots on his harmonica. His hands cradled the backside of the instrument. A knee-slapping, toe-tapping version of "Turkey in the Straw" filled the air.

"Wait," pleaded Pauline. "Let me play along with the spoons." She tightly clamped two spoons back to back between her index and ring finger. Laying them across her thigh, she clicked them together keeping time by the tapping of her toe. "

Mama, petite and round-faced, danced a jig on the uneven dirt floor.

When Daddy played "Barbry Allen," Mama insisted he put down his mouth organ to harmonize with her:

> *Was in the merry month of May*
> *When flowers were a bloomin',*
> *Sweet William on his death-bed lay*
> *For the love of Barbry Allen.*
> *Slowly, slowly she got up,*
> *And slowly she went nigh him,*
> *And all she said when she got there,*

"Young man, I think you're dyin'"

But, when there was corn liquor to make, all singing ceased at dark. For dark was the safest time to light the fire under Daddy's still.

One night, after sundown, Mama took the children into the corn patch. Hand in hand, they walked the narrow trail, winding through a maze of tall stalks to the edge of the dugout hollow surrounding Daddy's still.

Encircled by dry, rustling corn, the faces of her family glowed under a full moon overhead. Pauline sat cross-legged on the bare ground, engrossed in rubbing and picking at the calluses on her now rough, leathery hands, the only reminder of her cotton-picking days. Fading memories of painful fingertips at war with prickly branches and fine white remnants sticking to every part of her—tickling her nose with every breath—were quickly fading.

The flame of the fire and the constant dripping of liquid corn seemed to cast a spell on Pauline. She savored the warmth that came from somewhere deep inside, which was more than any flame could deliver. She folded her arms behind her neck and lay back, absorbed in the thin white trail of vapor stretching up to the ever-silent Man in the Moon.

* * * * *

Buying sugar for Daddy's business was nearly the sole purpose for the family's weekly trips to town. Pauline was grateful for the need. Sometimes Mama bought a loaf of bread with a balloon inside the wrapper. She kept a list in her pocketbook of who had earned a balloon and who had not. Even Delbert could barely wait until the lucky winner was announced. On the way home the balloon was repeatedly inflated and noisily sent on its way, darting wildly from one side of the car to the other. The children futilely grabbed at the air trying to capture the unpredictable target until the whole family burst into gales of laughter.

* * * * *

One Saturday morning, Pauline watched as Delbert examined an old clock given to him by Daddy.

"What makes it tick?" She asked, looking over his shoulder curiously. By the time he finally turned around to answer she was high stepping it to the house.

Later, Pauline approached Delbert again. She held out her tightly clutched fist. "Trade you this doll crier for that ol' clock?" She held her breath as Delbert inspected the piece.

"Deal," he said, as he began putting the clock parts into an old tobacco tin.

Back at the soddy, Pauline laid her newfound treasure under her bedroll until she could decide on a place to work.

When she was alone, she chose a private shaded spot at the back of the barn. She hit two old wooden boxes together, knocking the dirt off. Placing them side-by-side, she jostled them a little to make sure they were close to level. An old piece of siding, lying up against the chicken house, served as her worktable.

Legs folded beneath the wobbly setup, Pauline laid the box of clock parts to one side of her meager tool collection. Elbows leaning on the splintery wood, she placed her hands together in prayer position. As if to prolong the pleasure of the moment, she paused, looking out at the endless prairie before her to soak up the raw beauty.

Now and then, a gusty breeze stirred up a scent of rusty metal, tobacco and old wood. Pauline stashed the aroma away somewhere in the depths of her soul.

She was surprised at how quickly she could put the clock together and take it apart again. *Why does this come so easy for me?* She basked in a feeling of prideful satisfaction that surged through her—until she caught sight of June peering around the corner.

"What do you want, June?"

Leaning over Pauline's shoulder June asked, "What's been keeping you so busy over here, Paulinnnnne?" June's eyes narrowed as she quickly scanned the evidence. "Hey, thought that was Delbert's clock. What are you doing with it?"

"Oh, Delbert gave it to me."

"I think Mama better know about this. I can't believe Delbert would give up something he treasured as much as that clock!"

Pauline felt as if a heavy band was tightening around her forehead. "June, if you don't tell Mama I'll let you have a turn."

Pauline watched as June's backside rounded the corner. Carefully, she placed the clock back in its box. Pushing her tools to one side, she arranged them according to length. Then folded her hands and waited.

Cringing, she heard Mama and June shuffling toward her.

"Pauline."

"Yes, Mama."

"Tell me about what you have in that tobacco tin."

Pauline looked out at the prairie just as she had when she

started her project. The beauty and peacefulness now seemed ugly and desolate.

"Well, Mama this is a box of clock parts. It used to belong to Delbert, but he gave it to me."

"He gave it to you, Pauline?" Mama's eyebrows rose unevenly.

"Well, I traded him..." Pauline said, voice trailing.

"You traded him what?"

In the silence that followed, Pauline struggled to avoid Mama's stare. She shifted her eyes as if searching the corners of her mind for a good excuse, for stealing the crier out of June's doll.

Mama's face looked distorted as Pauline gazed into her eyes through tears on the verge of spilling. She struggled to keep her mouth straight and tight, but an annoying, quiver tugged at her chin controlling her lips like puppet strings. From out of nowhere came horrible gulping sobs. She felt her stomach pulsating hard against her ribs as she tried to control her wailing. As if peering through a rain gusher she could see the shocked expressions on Mama and June's faces.

At last, Mama cradled Pauline in her arms. "All you have to do is tell the truth, honey. All you have to do is tell the truth."

Pauline looked over at June's watery eyes and tight dimpled chin.

"June, I know how happy you were the day cousin Maggie handed that Cry-Baby Doll down to you." Between high pitched gasps for breath, she murmured; "Now she's torn and will never cry again."

June locked arms with Mama encircling Pauline. She pressed her silky cheek close to Pauline's ear, "At least you told the truth. I'm too old to play with dolls anyway."

* * * * *

Most Sunday afternoons, the Sampleys walked up the road to Uncle Charlie and Aunt Julia's. Their house was always bulging with people since Uncle John and his family lived nearby too.

The women, including June, set about frying freshly butchered chickens and putting together all the fixings. Meanwhile, the men carried sawhorses from the barn to the front porch. Then, they lifted the doors off Aunt Julia's root cellar and lay them across each stand.

Leaning against a porch post, Pauline stood in awe of the perfect motion of it all. Aunt Julia and Mama threw a clean white sheet high above the primitive tabletop, allowing it to float freely down. Pauline silently wished she was hunched down under that soft, fresh smelling fabric as it billowed and caught the air. A mysterious feeling of her past drifted before her, reminding her of something that may once have been.

The women continually chattered back and forth as they worked. Aunt Julia advised anyone inclined to listen, "I pour my wastewater from the dishes on to the garden. Every little bit helps when you're tryin' to raise a garden. Soap suds keep the bugs away too."

Mama bragged, "Jack figured out a way to get our shower water out to his corn patch. Lord knows it needs all the help it can get with this drought we've been having."

Pauline stood aloof, now leaning against the doorframe. *"Why do they do that? They straighten the tablecloth making sure the edges are even. They jerk and brush at wrinkles and creases without ever missing a word. There are some things about ladies that I swear I never will understand."*

After dinner, on July 2, 1932, the three families huddled around the radio. They listened intently to Franklin D. Roosevelt's campaign speech.

"I pledge you, I pledge myself, to a New Deal for the American People."

"And now, today's agricultural report: Cotton has dropped in price to five cents a pound. Wheat today is at fifty cents a pound."

The adults leaned in closer, their eyes peering intently yet staring at nothing.

A news correspondent relayed the day's Labor Report.

"It was reported early this morning that hourly wages in this country have dropped by sixty percent. In addition, twenty-five percent of the labor force is unemployed..."

Any laughter the radio produced during these times of hardship was usually brought about by the light-hearted attitude some took toward prohibition. Over the air came a piece written by one New York rhymester:

> *Mother's in the kitchen*
> *Washing out the jugs*
> *Sisters in the pantry bottling the suds;*
> *Father's in the cellar*
> *Mixing up the hops*
> *Johnny's on the front porch*
> *Watching for the cops.*

Will Rogers brought a smile to the faces of the adults when the announcer repeated his quote, "The worst crime a child can commit is to eat up the raisins that Dad brought home for fermenting purposes."

For Mama though, laughter concerning breaking the law was hard to come by. Only out of necessity had she agreed to let Daddy spend their hard earned savings for a copper still.

* * * * *

One Sunday evening, on the way home from Aunt Julia's, the Sampley children decided to play 'follow the leader'. They knew not to ask Daddy to play such a childish game, but Mama took very little begging to join in. Daddy threw his head back, laughing, at the sight of the motley group walking backward, sideways, skipping and then twirling until they staggered dizzily.

They were soon interrupted when off in the distance they spied a car coming fast toward them. It looked as if it didn't belong. Mama squinted and scowled, and began wringing her hands. The family clustered close together walking quickly in the direction of the soddy. The car pulled alongside and stopped. All at once Pauline's heart pounded, and her chin and knees began to quiver.

The man driving flashed Daddy a badge. "Harley Sampley, we're gonna have to take a look around." Both men tilted their felt brimmed hats with a quick nod. Pauline wondered why the man called Daddy 'Harley' Sampley when Mama always called him 'Jack.' *Umm, it's probably not a good sign.*

Mama looked straight into their eyes, unblinking. Pauline thought, *Oh no, it's the look we all hate—the 'I'm not backing down' look.*

Daddy spoke firmly, "Git on in the house kids, your Ma and I will take care of things."

Pauline's legs felt rubbery as she ran inside with the others. They all scrambled for a spot at the window. Dale and June watched, weeping softly. Delbert and Pauline glared, hands on hips, daring the man to touch one stalk of corn or one hair on Daddy's head. Their frustration grew, as the Feds searched the cellar and tore the beds and the car apart, then drove away empty handed. Pauline let her built-up anger fly, as she ran behind the agitators' car in a haze of whirling dust—screaming, "Ya Beelzebub's! Mama do ya think it was that mean ol' rooster that keep them from a searchin' the hen house?"

When their car was nearly out of sight, Pauline joined the others who stood huddled around Mama and Daddy.

"They didn't take you away, Daddy. We were so afraid."

Pauline looked up and saw that Mama's eyes were closed. She looked so soft and tender. Her folded hands were calm and still.

Walking back to the soddy together, Daddy asked, "Pauline, where did you ever hear the word 'Beelzebub'?"

"Mama taught it to me, Daddy. It's from the Bible. It means Devil."

"What a girl."

"At least she wasn't cussing, Jack," said Mama. Daddy reared his head back in laughter. "Yes, at least she wasn't cussing, Fay."

Later that night, when the children were all in bed, Daddy tried to explain what the future might hold.

"Ya know kids, up 'til now we've had the fixin's to, at least get along. But, without that ol' corn licker money, we're liable to really find out what poor is."

It'll take all of us pitching in just to keep food on the table. And to top it off, Ol' Mother Earth, she's turnin' against those folks who only takes and don't give nothin' back. She's gone and changed our soil to powder. The crops don't have nothin' to sink their roots into."

With a firm jaw Daddy looked at each of his children one by one. "Youngin's, we've bootlegged together, we've picked crops together, and we may be poor together, but one thing I'll promise you right now is that we'll always be together." He cupped his big strong hand around the kerosene lamp and blew out the flame.

Chapter Three

Pauline stretched herself over the rickety rails of the pigpen. She counted twelve newborn piglets—several latched on to a teat of the bulging sow. Some dozed, sliding down her belly and tucking in here and there—rising and falling in time with the sows labored breathing.

"What the Sam Hill," whispered Pauline. "I gotta tell the others."

Toe catching on the last fence board, she felt a stabbing, knocking her to the ground.

After Pauline gathered herself, she realized she was eye to eye with piglet number twelve who lay shivering from lack of its mother's warmth. Her fingertips felt the short, uneven pulse of its slick, bluish body. She rolled it in her shirttail, holding it close to her before climbing back over the fence.

The sight of Mama on her way back from the chicken house was an answer to her prayer. "Mama, come quick. The sow delivered."

"Pauline, don't you see that I am carrying a heavy basket of eggs here?"

"Mama, come—now! Somethin's not right."

Showing no fear for the delicate eggs, Mama sat the wire egg basket down and ran toward Pauline—her faded yellow apron flapping in the breeze.

"What's wrong?"

Pauline unwrapped the bulge snuggled in her shirttail, afraid the poor thing was dead, and if it was—she might just instinctively drop it, having never touched anything dead before.

"Mama, he must have been alone in that corner for who knows how long? He's warming up a bit, but what are we gonna do?"

Mama laid her palm on the piglet's belly between its short outstretched legs tipped with tiny hooves. "You're right Pauline. He's still alive, but barely. We'll put him by the woodstove while I'm cooking dinner. Wrap him up tight, keep him close to your body just like you were doing, and massage him to get his blood circulating." Pauline did as told.

While Mama busied herself starting the fire in the stove and preparing a bottle of milk, Pauline sat by the stove with her bundle. She held her thumb in the piglet's mouth as Mama instructed her so he would get used to sucking. We'll have to get something in the little runt soon, or else..." said Mama.

"That's a good name for him, Mama. I'll call him 'Runt.'"

In the weeks that followed, Pauline carried Runt around like June used to carry her doll. He waited by the door for her to come out in the morning. Then, he'd snort non-stop until his long, slobbery tongue fetched a treat from her dress pocket. It was a cute trick she had taught him when he was just a few weeks old, but it now left her with muddy, slimy streaks down the front of her dress. She held the thin cloth away from her body, waving it back and forth in the dry summer air.

When it wasn't too hot, Runt followed Pauline and Dale out into the prairie, looking for snakeskins, bird feathers, fossils, and bleached white cattle skulls. But Runt couldn't handle much heat.

One scorching day, Runt refused to stay back. No matter how many times she yelled, "Runt, git home," he continued to meander along behind her. *Maybe he'll be okay if we stay close to home,* thought Pauline. Caught up in exploring they wandered farther than intended. Pauline stared at Runt as he staggered, walking in circles. "Dale, come on, help me git him home to the water pump," she said in a panicked voice.

The two struggled to get a good grip on Runt's belly, leaving his legs dangling. They awkwardly sidestepped across the prairie—Runt snorting every step of the way.

Reaching the house, they plopped him under the water pump where Pauline attempted to hold him steady. Dale grunted as his thin arms lifted the stiff handle of the pump, thrusting it up and down until a slow, steady stream trickled out. Once a good size puddle formed, Pauline shouted, "Shut 'er down, Dale."

"Whew, can't cool him off too quick, 'cause that might be worse than nothin' at all."

Runt lay panting while the two splashed water on their faces. Then they both squatted, heads down, elbows on knees, red-faced, breathing heavy.

* * * * *

Mama had dropped plenty of hints that Runt was going to have to go. "Uncle Charlie and Aunt Julia are lookin' to buy some pork, Pauline." Mama conveniently kept the Sears catalog open to girls' dresses. "Look what you could buy from the sale, school dresses for you and June."

Pauline wrinkled her nose, "June?"

"Yes, to make up for what you did to her doll."

"No thanks, Mama, I'll just keep Runt."

Pauline's mind raced through two sleepless nights. I can't lift him anymore. He's bullied and burrowed his way into the chicken house, gorging himself on chicken feed, which Lord knows, can't be spared. The poor chickens won't go into their house at night for fear of Runt barging in and rooting them out of their nests. He's scaring the poor things to death making them take their chances against the coyotes by a-sittin' on the hood of the car, or in the hayloft.

In the past, Pauline had enjoyed the sound of coyotes howling in the night. Now she knew it was their celebration of what was to follow—the loud screaming and squawking of a hen being torn to pieces then—the dreaded silence.

At the first sign of daylight, Pauline scouted out a fresh pile of bloody feathers. She hollered his name in a loud whisper while digging a hole to bury the evidence, hoping that no one would notice the poor girl was missing and all the while knowing they would.

The war going on inside her was violent. To do right by her family, she would have to kill her best friend. How could she? How could she sell Runt to Uncle Charlie? She tried to rub the ripples from her forehead—her eyes burned.

Runt looked up at her with his beady, little, bloodshot eyes that Pauline always thought too small for his body. He pressed his body down beside her. She scratched him hard behind the ears.

Pauline thought it was annoying the way the whole family pretended not to notice the struggle she was having with her decision. *I know they want—me—to decide because they know how much he means to me. I wish Mama or Daddy would just make me give him up. They won't though, it's the way we Sampleys are. Mama would call it one of the hard lessons of life, ugh.*

After supper that night, Pauline spotted Runt lying against the shady side of the soddy. She sprawled prostrate next to his ear. "Runt, this is the hardest thing I have ever had to do. You're the first thing I ever saved from sure death. I love ya, Runt." She kissed him on the velvety spot just above his snout.

Head down and shoulders drooping, she walked toward the house followed by the sound of hooves hitting the ground behind her. She frowned at the sound of Runt's demanding snorting and pointed her finger at him, "No Runt, you stay!" Turning away, she ran to the soddy. Before opening the door she quickly wiped her face with the back of her arm, smearing dirt across her nose and forehead.

"Runt is ready to go, Mama. You're right, we have other animals to feed, and putting clothes on our backs is way more important than havin' a pet pig."

Pauline tucked herself into bed before supper that night. Hot tears rolled down her cheeks until after dark when she heard the rest of the family approaching the feed house. She quickly turned toward the wall pulling the quilt over her head and pressing it hard over her ears. There was no talking that night, and Pauline hated it when a lingering sob suddenly escaped her. She could almost touch the unspoken sorrow that had filled the air all around them.

* * * * *

On a Sunday morning, Daddy called a family meeting.

"Your Mama and I think we can pick up a little work in the wheat fields. We want you children back in school, so you'll learn to read and write like your Mama."

The groans came in unison, "Do we have to, Daddy?"

Mama tapped the air with her pointer finger as she spoke, "You have to use the brains God gave you for something besides picking cotton. Now, yes, I won't hear another word about it."

Pauline shuddered at the thought of starting back to school in the middle of the school year. *That surely will be worse than death itself. The other kids will stare at us. We'll be way behind in everything. I won't be able to stand it.*

Pauline took the risk of one last, well thought out, plea, "But, Mama, we can't go without shoes."

"We'll manage," Mama said firmly.

Pauline knew full well what that meant. The boys might have to wear girl's hand-me-down shoes or, worse yet, the other way around.

Mama kept her promise about the dresses from the Sears Catalog, although Pauline didn't much care, she thought it probably made Mama feel good.

Pauline chose a red dress even though June said it would clash with her red hair and make her freckles stand out. June, as if she was going to a ball, labored over her decision before choosing a pink dress with a white lace collar.

* * * * *

Pauline thought it suspicious that Mama would insist on making a fresh batch of lye soap just two days before they were due to start school. She watched Daddy carry the big cast iron kettle over near the garden and set it on three good-sized rocks. Mama heated about a gallon and a half of water and a can of lye, and then added plenty of meat waste.

With every batch she would say, "Stay away from this lye, it'll burn you like fire."

The concoction bubbled and boiled while Mama stirred it continuously with a long stick. Every once in a while, she scooped a little out to see if it had congealed yet. Mama said, "It should look just like jelly." When it was ready, she spread the mixture out and let it dry on a board, then covered it until morning. Pauline and June always looked forward to the task of cutting the soap into bars.

On Sunday before they were to start school, Mama insisted her children bathe and wash their hair. She heated a kettle of water on the wood stove. Each child knew to stand on the wood slats that Daddy had carefully leveled and placed on the south side of the soddy. Overhead hung a bucket with small nail holes in the bottom. It was one of Daddy's inventions.

When ready to bathe, the bucket was lowered with a rope attached to a pulley then filled from a pitcher of warm water, tied off, and fast as lightning you scrubbed all over. If you didn't have enough water to rinse off, the lye soap gave you a rash.

Pauline was resting on her haunches on the other side of the soddy when she heard June call out, "Pauliiiiinnnnneeeee, I need more water."

Pauline strolled slowly to June's aide, "Yes, what is it, June."

"I said I NEEEEEEED more water. I still have some soap in my hair.

"Weeeellll, June, you know Mama only allows one bucket for each of us."

"Ohhhhh Pauline, you are meaner than a wet hen! You never need all of your water anyway—can't you just give me some—please?"

"Well, I suppose I could since I happened to notice that your name is next on Mama's list for the bread wrapper balloon."

"Okay, Pauline, okay anything! Just give me the water!"

Before sunrise the next morning, Pauline was dreaming of golden wheat stretching as far as the eye could see. Faintly, somewhere off in the distance, she heard Daddy's voice. "Come on baby, time to get up, gotta get dressed."

"Oooooh Daddy I can't, I just can't."

"Oh yes, you can. And to boot, you and June will be two of the prettiest girls at school today in them fancy new dresses."

Pulling her dress down over her head, Pauline breathed in the pleasing, starchy scent of newness. The sisters awaited Mama's approval while she circled them—just like the cloth on Aunt Julia's table that Sunday, she brushed and tugged, and finally stood back, hands on hips, with a sigh and a smile. "There girls, you're both pretty as pictures."

Pauline knew full well that the only similarity between June and herself was their identical bowl haircuts—cut by Daddy the night before. Daddy was good at cutting hair. He found that Mama's green mixing bowl fit almost perfect around the hairline of the four youngsters. All he had to do was trim around the edge. It was only when they shivered from the hair tickling their face that made it look uneven. They knew what Daddy meant when he said, "Oops, hold still now, baby—oh well, it'll grow."

Pauline remembered gathering the hair clippings and throwing them out behind the barn for birds to rummage through. It was a favorite pastime to look for strains of hair carefully woven into nests amidst pieces of hay and Mama's sewing scraps that were thrown out behind the barn, too. Pauline was the only one who could positively stake out part ownership of a birds nest, being the only one with red hair.

* * * * *

Standing in front of the schoolhouse, the children watched nervously, as Mama and Daddy drove away. Pauline looked at her siblings. June's thick, dark hair shined, but her forehead was creased with worry. Pauline gave her the once-over. "You look purty in pink, June."

Suddenly she knew the reason for June's worry. She had on horrid boys' shoes that were at least two sizes too big, with cardboard stuffed in the toes.

Delbert, chin taut, seemed ready to handle anything the day might bring on. *Mama must have given up on trying to tame his cowlick.*

Pauline glanced down thoughtfully and realized Dale was wearing her shoes from last year. *That explains why he irritated everyone on the way to the car this morning, lagging behind, dragging his shoes. Poor little guy, he was trying to scrape the heels off—trying to make them look more like boys' shoes.* She clutched his hand tightly as if to protect him from any humiliation the day might bring.

Pauline chose a desk close to the back of the room. Stomach churning, she prayed that the teacher wouldn't ask her anything.

"Good morning, students," said Miss Platte in a low, gruff voice. "Starting with this very dirty little boy in the row by the window, call out your names one at a time for my roll sheet. Begin."

The class watched as the boy slumped into his chair. He looked down at the scarred desktop in front of him and mumbled, "Herbert."

Miss Platte walked over and quickly put one finger under the tip of the boy's chin. "Herbert, always look at me when I am talking to you, and speak up."

Miss Platte slowly moved between the rows of mismatched desks, tapping each with her ruler as she passed. Pauline swallowed over and over again trying to come up with some spit to quench her thirst. She flinched as Miss Platte's ruler came down on the desk just a few inches from her arm. Quickly, Pauline looked up into the teacher's narrow, squinty eyes trying to ignore the tight, wrinkled pucker of her lips.

Pauline tried to say her name loud and clear, but she was shocked to hear only a raspy hint of a voice. After another click of the ruler, she blurted out, "Pauline." Miss Platte frowned and moved on, heels echoing on the loose wood slats of the floor.

Later, out on the playground, the Sampley children gathered around June as she dished up cold beans from the rusty, metal lunch bucket Mama had packed. She then handed each a piece of bread. They leaned back against the cool foundation of the well house and whispered about Miss Plate as they ate. Delbert spoke in a grown-up, fatherly voice, "Just mind your own business and listen up, and you'll be okay. I hope." He chuckled nervously causing the others to giggle.

Looking around the schoolyard Pauline noticed a girl, about her age, sitting alone. The girl was thin, hair oily and stringy. She didn't have a lunch bucket like the others. Several times she walked across the yard to pump water into a cup hanging from a rope. Pauline tried not to stare at the girl's protruding muscle trembling as she pushed down on the stiff handle of the pump. She watched her gulp the water down as if to fill an empty stomach.

Pauline elbowed June. "June, did you see that girl? I feel like giving her some of my lunch."

"Yes, I saw her, Pauline. But you go giving your lunch away and you'll be looking just like her before long."

"It's so pitiful," Pauline sighed with a gentle shake of her head.

When the school bell rang, Pauline made sure she was next to the girl as everyone lined up for class. "What's your name?" For a fleeting moment, she noticed the otherwise dull eyes of the pale-faced girl brighten.

"Claire," said the girl in a feeble voice. They both smiled, knowingly.

Back in class, Pauline realized that Claire was seated right behind her. Miss Platte had just finished writing some arithmetic problems on the board when Pauline overheard Claire breathing heavily. Realizing she had fallen asleep, Pauline sat frozen, fearful of causing Miss Platte to look in the girl's direction.

With a sigh, chalk in hand, Miss Platte announced: "Since we have four new students today, I will have to take the time to re-evaluate the skills of the whole class. We will probably have two low skill groups since so many of you fall into that category." A low moan could be heard. "No use complaining, it's the penalty we pay when people start in the middle of the school year." Her sharp, gruff voice mellowed as she walked softly, mostly on her toes, toward the back of the room.

Pauline stared at the chalkboard, then at the book in front of her. A deafening crack of the ruler came down hard on Claire's desk, startling the whole class. Pauline turned around in time to see Miss Plates pinched face—veins in her neck throbbing—her thin body hovering over Claire.

Pauline saw the horror in Claire's bulging eyes as she sat on the edge of her chair, lips quivering. She looked straight into Pauline's eyes. Pauline knew the shame Claire was suffering was far worse than any bodily pain could ever be. She felt Claire's hurt burn deep down inside.

Later in the afternoon, walking home from school, Pauline and the others relived their day. Dale, still dragging his feet in the hope of scraping off any remaining telltale signs of girls' shoes, listened intently. "Wait 'til Mama hears," he stammered.

"I won't have it, Jack. This is learning? We'll take the children to the wheat fields with us. I can teach them at home after work."

Daddy nodded agreeably, "After all, Fay. You taught school fer three years fore we moved here. They'd be hard-pressed to find a better teacher."

* * * * *

The Sampleys arrived for work early. They crept into a small storage building near the wheat fields. Pauline blinked to focus in the dark smoky room. As her vision cleared, she recognized many of the hunched shoulders of the field workers. They stood tightly clustered around a bulky radio producing noisy, ear-piercing bursts of static. Mama and Daddy edged in close, pulling the children to them with a sense of urgency. Pauline could tell it wasn't going to be a morning for the usual roughhousing amongst the children. She felt Daddy's hands settling on her shoulders. *Yep, there will be no roughhousing today.*

Pauline studied the shoes of those nearby. With the toe of her shoe, she drew the letter P in the soft dirt floor. The folks standing in front of her shifted. She could see a man sitting on a chair with a cigarette tight between his lips. He slowly turned the knob on the radio, one ear cocked toward the speaker.

Suddenly, the static cleared and the newscaster's voice came in loud and clear, "Today, November 8, 1932, Franklin D. Roosevelt has won the presidential race by a landslide victory! Carrying the votes of all but six states, he is our new President of the United States. And he promises to restore this country to prosperity. His stunning defeat over President Hoover comes at a time when the nation is in bread lines and soup kitchens, of bank failures, farm foreclosures, and soaring unemployment. Despite the fact he is badly crippled from polio, he was buoyant, joyous and confident as he spoke of what he called a 'New Deal for Americans.'"

The adults in the crowd cheered throwing their fists high into the air. The radio played Roosevelt's campaign theme song "Happy Days Are Here Again." Pauline joined the children running around hollering and kicking up dust.

* * * * *

Night after night, the same sweet, predictable ritual took place with nary a complaint.

After the dinner dishes were cleared from the table, the four siblings sat around the kitchen table pencils in hand, waiting for Mama to give them their lesson assignments. Each had work that had been prepared by Mama—they never knew when. Once each child was well on their way, Mama would pull one aside for individual practice and quizzing. This was the part everyone looked forward to when they had Mama's attention all to themselves.

With a piece of Mama's time devoted just to her—Pauline began to feel that schoolwork wasn't so bad after all. Correct answers on tests were met with an unrestrained show of pride from Mama and the others. Hands flew up, slapping down hard on knees, and smiles stretched across all faces.

Chapter Four

It was late afternoon at the wheat field in the year 1934. The sun had beat down for weeks at a time with no rain in sight. Pauline propped her oversized broom up against a knothole in the barn siding. On her knees, she scraped a small pile of wheat into the palm of her hand and dropped the kernels into one of Daddy's old tobacco tins. She surveyed the area with a critical eye. "There, the boss will have nothin' to gripe about and Mama's chickens will eat tonight."

Pauline stood on the threshold of the barn looking out toward what had been golden, glistening wheat. *Why does the wheat look so dull and dirty today?* She frowned up at the darkening sky studying small patches of dust swirling into funnels. "Mama," she called, "Why does everything look so strange?"

Mama examined the skies too as if searching for an answer.

As they made their way home, the wind howled and spat sand hard against the rolled up windows of the Oakland. By the time they arrived, the sky was nearly as black as night.

Daddy pulled the car up next to the cellar, and together Delbert and Daddy battled the harsh wind. They struggled to lift the already half-buried doors as the wood planks bowed and creaked against the pounding storm.

In the midst of the dark, musty cellar, Daddy inched his hands along the top of the tabletop until he found a candle. Then all at once, his face shone from the soft, flickering light. Daddy's reassuring smile and outstretched arms invited Pauline to mold herself into the crook of his arm and the crevice of his neck.

Daddy's thin arms embraced Pauline. He held her humming and swaying back and forth to the slow rhythm of "The Old Rugged Cross." *On a hill away, there's an Old Rugged Cross, the emblem of suffering and shame.*

Pauline looked up into Daddy's eyes. She remembered when they were once electric blue. Now they appeared two colorless gray stones separated by deep creases and underlined with dark circles. He stroked her hair, catching strains now and then on his rough, split fingertips.

Pauline eyed the inside of the cellar for the first time since they had taken cover. She had always shuddered at the sight of the two weathered doors lying at an angle against the soddy. Talk of "going to the cellar" made her think of rats the size of her leg, waiting to scurry across bare toes, or huge poisonous spiders stuck to her hair by sticky webs.

The wind whistled while forcing fitful gusts of sand through cracks in the heaving doors overhead. Pauline shook her head slowly as she saw Mama's canned goods trembling on a rickety shelf against one wall. Carrots, potatoes, and onions lay on a screen of chicken wire. Spider webs swung erratically from the corners of the dugout.

In the days that followed, the webs were swept from the cellar weekly. A lantern was hung just inside the door.

Mama preached about tying a wet handkerchief over your mouth to prevent the fine, talcum powder-like dust from clogging your lungs.

When the winds came, Mama knew the difference between the black dust from Oklahoma, the gray dust from Kansas, and the brown dust from New Mexico. The dark, thick blizzards seemed hungry for what remained of a country down on one knee from dust depression.

Two days later, Pauline sat cross-legged on the dirt against a lean-to up against the barn. She trickled water from her pail onto the sand in the form of a figure eight, tamping the spongy sand until it was firm and level. Using small chunks of wood for cars, she drove them up and down her newly-formed road while creating a gravelly, humming sound.

From a distance, Pauline heard Mama holler, "Head to the cellar, kids."

Already beginning to choke on the dense air, Pauline dipped her handkerchief in the water trough as she ran passed. No time to worry about the green slime floating on top. Out of the corner of her eye, she noticed Daddy attempting to herd Nellie and Ol' Dan to the barn. She stopped to help him, flapping her arms up and down behind the animals.

Daddy shouted, "Pauline, you git on to the cellar, now."

She obeyed, struggling to wring out the dripping cloth and tie it over her mouth and nose. She leaned into the wind, ignoring the burn of the blowing sand stinging every part of her that wasn't clothed. She stepped over the top of a barbed wire fence, now sticking out of a newly created dune.

Earlier in the day, Pauline had noticed Nellie and Ol' Dan standing close—sides pressed against each other. In the back of her mind, she had questioned their silent voices—their ears rotating from side to side, sometimes one upright and one flat. They spoke what Pauline could not hear—a storm was on the way.

With everyone safe in the cellar, Pauline watched with gnawing uneasiness as Daddy's chest heaved back and forth, gasping for air. She saw the worried look in Mama's eyes.

Mama scolded, "Jack, you have to keep that dust from getting down into your lungs. That can't be good, and you know it. Look at you! You can hardly catch your breath. If the animals stray, then it was meant to be."

"Fay, I ain't a gonna leave Nellie and Ol' Dan out in this. They've been there fer us when we needed them."

Pauline patted Mama on the forearm, "Mama, did you see what happened?"

"No, I don't suppose I did, Pauline."

"The chickens, Mama, when the sky grew dark, they thought it was night. They ran to the chicken house to roost. They ran as fast as their skinny little stick legs could carry them, straight into the hen house." The whole family burst into bellyaching laughter.

Delbert, hand pushed hard against his stomach as if somehow that would help him catch his breath, added, "Looked a lot like Dale running to the cellar, huh, Pauline?" Another gale of soul-cleansing laughter slowly gave way to quiet.

Pauline turned her head to one side listening. "The wind has stopped."

* * * * *

Pauline had come to dread pulling into the lane after work each night. The hungry gaze of Nellie and 'Ol Dan was almost more than she could bear. Her gut wrenched at the sight of their protruding ribs and soft, questioning eyes. Pressing her cheek firmly against Ol' Dan's nose, she massaged his withers. His head dropped lower and lower as if he were in a trance.

Pauline's voice cracked, "Why do you stay? Your fence is somewhere under a heap of sand. Why don't you just take off?"

She remembered Daddy in days past near huge stacks of tumbleweed piled against fencerows. "Pauline, why would God create such a shallow rooted nuisance"?

Even though she knew Daddy didn't expect an answer, she replied anyway, "Mama says God has a reason for everything, and we will find out in His time, not ours."

"That's my girl. You sound jest like your Mama!"

The next day before leaving the field, the workers gathered at the office to swap stories about farms buried by dust and whole towns black as coal. They listened to the radio blare the news of the rest of the world and, of course, the local weather.

"The county farm report thus far shows a value of $7,000 spread among 800 farmers compared with a past study showing a profit of almost $1.2 million. And now today's weather report: For tomorrow and the rest of the week, once again, no rain in sight. Possible high winds expected."

* * * * *

Pauline sat on an overturned bucket next to the water-pump watching Daddy sharpen his razor, scraping the pearl-handled blade back and forth on a thick leather strap.

"Look 'ere, Pauline. This razor, shaving brush, and strap, is the only things I have that belonged to my Daddy."

Pauline wet the brush and rubbed it around and around a bar of soap before handing it to Daddy.

"What was your Daddy like?" She asked.

"Believed in hard work. Didn't think much of schoolin'. Used to say, 'The best way to learn is by doin',' and 'Common sense is what counts.' Any of his kids misbehaved, they felt the sting of this 'ere strap on their backsides."

Daddy handed Pauline the shaving brush, "Get some more soap on there, Runt."

Swirling the soft hairs of the brush around and around until a sudsy lather formed she questioned, "Why ya shavin' today, Daddy? It's not Saturday."

"No it's not Saturday, but a man jest feels better when he's clean shavin'. Pauline, the way things been goin' lately, I have a hunch that today jest' might be our last day a work."

"Ya mean the boss might let us go today?"

"Yep, and your Daddy's got his pride ya know."

"I know, Daddy, I know."

I wonder if the others are a thinkin' the same thing?

Pauline leaned against the car waiting for her family to file out of the soddy. Turning her face toward the sky, her nostrils flared. She inhaled the nauseating scent of an approaching dust storm.

In the past, the wheat fields had called Pauline to them—an endless carpet of feathers swaying in perfect harmony—their song barely heard. Lately though, Pauline felt uneasy about the growing bare patches amidst stiff, dry stems. Even a slight breeze brought forth an abrasive, crackling sound.

Halfway to the fields, Pauline could see that Mama was nervously tapping her foot on the floorboard and twiddling her thumbs.

"Jack, that huge dust storm off in the distance looks like black smoke. It's headed right for us. It's the Lord, shaking a dusty fist at those who tilled the soil to feed themselves, never giving a thought to us poor souls trying to make a living off the remains. You know, Jack, when banks all over the country closed down you and I never gave it a thought. We never had cause to set foot in a bank a day in our lives. But this, Jack, this?"

"Maybe it'll let up by the time we get there, Fay."

When they pulled in front of the office, Mama shook her head sorrowfully as she saw a stream of cars pulling away.

Pauline whined, "Daddy, look at all the cars leaving."

"I would say that's not a good sign, Runt, not a good sign at all."

A gust of wind caught the door to the office building, slamming it back against the wall as if announcing their arrival. Grim-faced, the field boss stood before them. He hesitated then glanced down at a slender stack of bills sitting on the counter. "Sorry, Jack, after today there'll be no work. Guess Mother Nature's havin' her way." As he spoke, he nervously rolled a few bills together in a tight roll—*Probably to make it look like more,* thought Pauline. He shoved the roll into Daddy's hand. With a knowing nod, Daddy led his family toward the door.

"We knowed it'd only be a matter of time, good luck to ya now."

Before leaving they hesitated by the radio at the sound of President

Roosevelt's voice: "Togetherness would reverse the panic. The only thing we have to fear is fear itself."

"You hear that, kids, together, we Sampleys don't have nothin' to be afraid of. Yes sir, I know that just as sure as I know my name," said Daddy—shoulders back and head high.

* * * * *

Each day Daddy drove to town looking for odd jobs.

One day Mama called Pauline to her, "Pauline, run out to the hen house and get me a dozen eggs. Your Daddy can sell them in town for 10 cents, enough for a gallon of gas."

Pauline walked on her tiptoes, zigzagging back and forth across the henhouse floor—missing most of the slimy droppings. The stench rose with waves of heat. She used her hiking stick for balance and to pry the girls off their nests.

The last hen protectively glared and pecked at Pauline's stick, ruffling her feathers and squeezing herself deeper into the nest. A loud, screechy cackle announced the possible delivery of a fresh egg produced from one of the others.

Pauline labored to pry one side of the black and white speckled hen up to check her hunch, yes, one large, brown egg. Inch by inch, Pauline forced the stick under the girl's belly until suddenly she awkwardly flapped her wings and descended to the floor. Caught off guard, Pauline stepped back, flat-footed onto a pile of mushy, manure. "Yuck, you dad-burned turkey buzzard."

Pauline gently layered the eggs into her straw-lined basket before placing it in the Oakland next to Daddy. Watching him drive away she thought to herself, *Doggone it, Daddy's been looking for work in town for weeks now, and all he comes back with is egg money.*

The next morning, Pauline listened as Mama and Daddy sat at the table sipping coffee.

"Ya know, Fay. I never thought I'd see the day a man couldn't find a decent day's work. I believe it jest may be smarter to stay home and save the gasoline." Mama nodded as Daddy continued, "Today, I saw a woman down on her knees in the middle of Main Street. Right out loud she was a prayin', 'Dear Lord! Please give us another chance.' And you know the sad part of it? I was tempted to kneel right down beside her." The grim faces of the children shifted to laughter as they caught sight of Daddy's crooked grin.

Each morning, Pauline swept the roof of the soddy to keep it from caving in under the weight of the shifting sand drifts. Pauline, Mama, and June hung wet blankets over the doors and windows to trap some of the invasive grime that was sure to creep through the cracks and crevices.

Nightly, Mama passed out wet handkerchiefs to put over their faces while they slept. Morning revealed silhouettes on pillows—outlined by a dirty mist.

One day, Pauline carefully gripped a piece of coiled barbed wire tightly in her hand. She searched the open prairie until she saw a streak of dust disappear into a hole. Then she twisted the wire deep inside the hollow until she could turn no more. With a good hard yank, she proudly evicted a good-sized jackrabbit, or "Hoover Hog," as Daddy called them. "Here's dinner," she called out to herself. "Daddy sure doesn't think much of President Hoover."

* * * * *

As soon as Daddy came in the door, Mama eagerly sat down across from him. "Jack, I just got word that your brothers are pulling up stakes and moving out to California. They heard tell that there's plenty of work in the Golden State. Lord knows we can't blame them for going. It will be lonely without them though — their windmill over there spinning and clattering without a soul around to hear it.

"Anyway, Jack, they're having a Depression Party before they leave. The families from the wheat fields and all our neighbors from miles around are invited. Everyone will bring whatever food and drink they have on hand. Julia is going to fry up what's left of her chickens. There will be matchstick poker, music, and dancing. My only concern is you, Jack, do you think you'll feel up to going? You've been coughing so lately."

"Sure — I want to go, Fay, wouldn't miss it fer the world. It's been a long time since we Sampleys have been to a hoedown — too long. If I git to coughin' bad, I'll jest amble into the house and rest a bit."

"Oh, thank you, Daddy!" Pauline cried out as if speaking for all four of the beaming faces of the eavesdroppers.

Pauline's words seemed to come out an octave or two higher than normal, "Mama, would you please sew us up some new dresses for the party from those blue and yellow flowered feed sacks you have stashed away?" Mama sat up straighter and pursed her lips. Pauline talked faster and raised her voice another pitch. "I think June and I could sew all the straight seams Mama and..."

* * * * *

Pauline stood on the sidelines of the dance floor in her blue and yellow flowered dress. She studied each member of the band in awe. *They're all folks we've worked with in the fields.*

Hank, the fiddler, eyes closed, leaned way back—then down low, as beads of sweat broke out on his forehead.

Slim plucked the taut strings strung from a broom handle to an overturned washtub. He seemed spellbound by the deep throbbing beat it produced.

Shorty had his harmonica perched on a wire stand nestled around his neck. He took big gulps of air before drawing his lips tight over the perforated metal. As he reached the end of his breath on a high wavering note, his dark, bushy eyebrows slid high over partially closed eyes, causing a wave of deep creases to gather on his forehead. Banjo hanging below his waist, he strummed it furiously, his body standing perfectly still and emotionless.

Caught up in the sights and sounds, Pauline felt she would burst if she didn't let the rhythm that was welling up inside her find a way out. Her feet began to move like Mama's when she danced on the dirt floor of the soddy. She brushed the balls of each foot out against the floor and back with a hop, lifting her knees high. Her head and shoulders nodded while her arms dangled at her side.

Lost in her own world, Pauline turned sharply, her green eyes flashing, when she felt a tap on her shoulder. In front of her was a boy with freckles and a mop of thick, red hair shooting forth in all directions. *I've never seen so many freckles in one place,* she thought.

He spit out the words, "Wo-wo-wo-would ya li-like to d-d-dance?"

Pauline's already warm face became burning hot. She noticed her hair and the back of her dress was wet with sweat.

The last thing Pauline wanted was to dance with a boy, but his face appeared frozen with the fear of rejection, and his body tense to withstand the pain of it. Pauline felt certain a "No, thank you." might cause him permanent damage—possibly scarring him for life.

Pauline bit her lip and said, "Okay," but ignored his outstretched hand. She had always taken pride at her sense of rhythm, but now, she felt stiff as a board. The boy took her hand holding it so tight that there was no way he wouldn't feel the dampness of her sweaty palms that felt like suction cups clinging to him—causing her to sweat even more.

The red-haired boy faked a yawn, covering his mouth with his hand. Then smoothly slipped his arm around Pauline's waist, pulling her close. *Ugh. Why did they have to play a slow song now?* She kept her lower body well away from him, which left her with no clue as to which direction he would lead. Upon placing her arm on the boy's shoulder, Pauline felt the waist of her dress rising to her upper midriff. Embarrassed, she complained to herself, *Great! Now my knees are showing. I hate the feel of the peach fuzz on his cheek. His hair smells like straw.*

On the way home the family began to relive the evening. Pauline held her breath, hoping no one would say anything about her dancing with a boy. She knew they couldn't help but notice the horrible sight. Before anyone had time to bring up the dreaded subject, the conversation was squelched by Daddy's nagging cough.

Several days later, the Sampleys stood at the edge of the road, waving goodbye to Uncle John, Uncle Charlie, and their families as they drove past—their familiar possessions secured to the car by a mess of rope. Their smiles appeared frozen on trembling lips.

When the cars were out of sight, the family walked back to the homestead, arm in arm, in deafening silence.

* * * * *

Daddy's croupy cough was unrelenting. Even Mama's most reliable remedy of Horehound Candy dissolved in moonshine failed to offer relief. Mama complained that she needed a fresh lemon to make him some hot lemon juice to break up the mucus.

As if for the first time, Pauline noticed Daddy's belt was a couple of notches tighter, and his pants gathered at the waist. His unbuttoned shirt draped open revealed the shocking sight of his ribs and the heaving of his chest.

Out of instinct, Mama knew it was time for the Sampleys to move on. For the first time, since Pauline could remember, Mama took charge of their wellbeing. Daddy was too sick to be proud.

"We'll go to my cousin's in Nebraska, just until we can get ourselves back on our feet again, of course," Mama said with perfect posture and a clear determined voice. "I know they will give us a hand."

Daddy sat on the edge of a wooden chair that sat lopsided on the uneven dirt floor. His trembling fingers hid his face.

* * * * *

When a buyer came for the chickens, and Nellie and Ol' Dan, Pauline lay on her mat with her knees drawn tight against her chest. She crawled all the way under the covers, breathing in the familiar scent of sweat, straw, and Runt. *I miss my dear little Runt.* In her steamy nest she hummed "Amazing Grace," loudly, for fear of hearing one of the mules whinny or a hen cluck.

That night, by the light of a kerosene lamp, Mama sat tenderly holding her Mother's hand-painted Treasure Chest on her lap. For the last time in their soddy, the only home Pauline had ever known, Mama opened the box and took out the Bible and the Lavaliere.

Pauline timidly asked, "Mama, may I please hold the Lavaliere, just while you are reading?"

"Yes, sweetheart," Mama said, brushing Pauline's hair back out of her eyes. "Now, hold it gently. It's very fragile. It belonged to your grandmother you know."

Pauline gently stroked the small ruby and dangling pearl on it's tarnished gold chain.

"I know, Mama, I know."

Mama sighed, her breath quivering as she read. *But he knoweth the way that I take when he hath tried me, I shall come forth as gold.* Job 23:10.

Chapter Five

In the winter of 1935, Pauline stared as they passed abandoned homesteads one after the other. Her brow furrowed at the sight of families journeying along the road, gaunt and dazed, pushing baby buggies overflowing with their possessions. She couldn't help but smile at the sight of two burros towing a broken down car with three kids squeezed into the rumble seat. *What was life like for them before? Did they have a Nellie and Ol 'Dan or a Runt by another name? Did they crouch in a cellar with the wind a howlin' overhead and dust a siftin' in? Did those kids have ta go to school? Did their Mama read the Bible to them every night?*

The Sampleys pressed on in silence—no laughing, no jumping up and down, no balloons—only the sound of the rope, securing their belongings, thumping against the roof overhead. The wind pushed in through the rolled down windows. Daddy's worrisome cough seemed never-ending.

Pauline struggled to read an upcoming road sign, "You are now en-en-en..."

"Entering," said Mama.

"You are now entering the State of Nebraska," read Pauline proudly.

Pauline's skin crawled, and her legs ached. She was beginning to feel like a butterfly in a steel cocoon. She longed to arch her back and stretch her arms and legs.

Mama sat with Cousin Opal's letter on one knee and the map on the other. "Now, Jack, Cousin Opal writes that we should turn right by Al's Corner Store."

Pauline strained to look over Mama's shoulder, "Her writing is all squiggly, and it looks old. Are your cousins old?" Interrupting herself, Pauline shouted, "There! There's the store, Daddy."

As they turned down the tree-lined street, Daddy slowed the car to a crawl.

Mama read on, "Says here the address is 112 Poplar Street. You children watch for a sign."

Pauline, Delbert, and Dale hung over the front seat of the car. Heads together they canvassed the neighborhood.

June sat tall, back straight, and legs crossed at the ankles. Pauline, not able to resist imitating her, held her head high while flipping the tip of her nose up with her index finger and pursing her lips into a snobbish pucker.

Pauline whispered to herself, "I never thought it would look like this, houses in a row just like a field of corn. And a tree—every house has a tree."

Pauline shouted, "112, there it is!"

Daddy had no sooner shut off the engine than two white-haired ladies were seen peeking out from behind a frayed lace curtain covering the front window. Slowly the door opened, and the two came down the steps, clutching the handrail. Mama and her cousins stood in a circle for the longest time, hugging and firmly patting each other on the back.

Then, Mama turned toward her family—arms still linked—"Sampleys, meet your cousins, Pearl and Opel." She drew them close as they nodded shyly.

The cousins led the way through the house and up a steep, narrow stairway to a spacious, unfinished attic. Rafters peaked high in the middle, but it was necessary to crouch at the sides. Long, narrow, windows on each end sent distorted beams of sunlight across the wooden floor. Lining one wall were old trunks, books, a Victrola, and several yellowed, lace dresses.

Later that night, Mama and June arranged their bedrolls. Daddy, Pauline, and the boys carried the rest of their necessities up, placing each person's bundle of clothing at the foot of their bed.

Pauline noticed how carefully Mama lifted the family Bible out of its hinged treasure chest, checking to make sure the Lavaliere was still in place. "May I hold the Lavaliere, Mama?" Pauline asked as she gently lifted the ornate piece off of Mama's forefinger. She ran her fingers around the intricate nooks and crannies, dreamily laying it over the lid of the chest. Then she dangled it in front of the kerosene lamp, watching intently as the light shifted across the tiny ruby.

Mama read Isaiah 26:9. *With my soul have I desired Thee in the night; yea, with my spirit within me will I seek Thee early: for when Thy judgements are in the earth, the inhabitants of the world will learn righteousness.*

That night Pauline lay awake staring at the moonlight dimmed by the newspapers they had taped over the attic windows. "Mama, why does Daddy call newspapers 'Hoover blankets'?"

"Well, you see Pauline, some folks aren't as fortunate as we Sampleys. We still have The Oakland and a roof overhead. This very night, some folks are sleeping on the streets, blaming their hard luck on ex-President Hoover, their only protection against the elements are old newspapers used as blankets. Lord knows they're old newspapers, because they sure as sin can't afford new ones."

* * * * *

The next day, a lady in a white coat opened the door to the waiting room. "Mr. Sampley, the doctor will see you now."

Mama and the children marched through the doorway behind Daddy, ignoring the nurse's comment about the small examining room.

The doctor pressed his stethoscope tight against Daddy's chest. Pauline tried to read his eyes for some clue, but he soberly stared off into space as if eye contact might affect his diagnosis. Leaning against the cold gray wall with the others, Pauline became engrossed in watching Mama nervously twist and untwist one corner of her embroidered handkerchief.

The doctor raised his brows, squeezing them together as he glanced from Daddy to Mama. "Dust pneumonia," he announced somberly. He turned and mumbled something to the nurse, who had been standing like a white statue with her starched hat, crisp uniform, and stubby-heeled shoes.

Pauline heard Mama whisper something about Jesus and recognized the familiar glimmer of determination that seemed to have come over her.

* * * * *

Mama had never learned to drive—there was little money for gas anyway. On Sundays, she and the children walked five miles to the hospital. One unusually warm Sunday, they all arrived back at 112 Poplar with parched throats and swollen feet. When they opened the front door, the cousins were sitting with straight backs and folded hands on their Queen Anne chairs with a small lace-covered table between them.

Pearl cleared her throat, "Please sit. Make yourselves comfortable." They poured glasses of ice water from a sweaty pitcher.

Like rag dolls, Mama and June slithered onto their chairs while Delbert, Dale, and Pauline sat Indian style on the floor.

"Opal and I were just discussing our small flock of chickens. Just the two of us can't make a dent in all those eggs. We would just like to say-ahem, Fay, you are welcome to all the eggs you can use."

Mama held her chest with one hand, appearing faint, "It's the best gift we've received in a long time. We are truly obliged."

As the family climbed the stairs to the attic, Pauline wondered fleetingly, *Are the cousins feeling sorry for us?* Mama's words forced the unsettling thought from her mind, "Yes, the good Lord is watching out for us Sampleys. He surely is."

The next morning, since Pauline was the first up, Mama sent her to the hen house, hollering after her, "I need 12 eggs for each Angel Food Cake."

Pauline shouted back, "Ma, I can't make that happen?"

With anticipation, she climbed a nearby tree in search of just the right limb—one born with a fork for prying stubborn hens off their nests.

She was about to step out of the henhouse when she heard the dreaded sound of Simon's high-pitched crow. She slammed the door shut, pushing back against it, sucking in the putrid air of the foul-smelling retreat. She screamed at the top of her lungs while holding her nose, "Maa, Maaaaaaaaaaaaa."

The rooster crowed triumphantly. The thump of his wings beating down hard against his sides caused her to shudder. She envisioned him strutting back and forth on the other side of the door, chest puffed, head high.

"Pauline, open the door," said Mama impatiently.

Pauline gathered the courage to open it just enough to focus one eye on Mama, dwarfed by the upright broom in her hand.

"Where's Simon?" Pauline asked between short, panicky puffs.

"Simon is right where he always is when he sees the sight of this broom. Which brings up another question. Pauline, how many times have I told you to always take a broom with you when you go to the hen house? Girl, when will you ever learn to listen?"

Pauline grabbed the handle of her wire egg basket heaped with brown eggs carrying it with both hands. She leaned back letting her body absorb some of the weight. "Um, the cousins must not have gathered eggs for a while."

Pauline walked nervously with her head pivoting and eyes scanning the terrain.

"Whew, sorry Mama, guess I just forgot since he didn't appear to be anywhere in sight."

"Oh no, he's too smart for that, Pauline."

After the cousins had finished in the kitchen, Mama busied herself baking Angel Food cakes.

That afternoon, Pauline and the others went door-to-door selling and taking orders for 50 cents each.”

Later in the evening, Mama hung her apron over the knob on the pie safe and attempted to brush a day's worth of wrinkles off her dress. Chin high and jaw tight, she turned to close the kitchen door against the chilly night air.

“Time for bed. You'll need your rest as I've enrolled you all in school. You'll begin tomorrow morning.”

The gasps that followed caused Mama no more than a glance over her shoulder. “Run along, now. I'll be up shortly.”

The four climbed the stairs grumbling under their breath, “But it's the middle of the school year—again,” said Delbert.

Everyone except June chimed in.

“We're gonna stick out like sore thumbs,” groaned Dale.

“It's not fair,” whined Pauline.

✼ ✼ ✼ ✼ ✼

The teachers didn't seem to know where to put the Sampley children, or any of the children of farm laborers, for that matter. Pauline hoped the others didn't hear as the frazzled teacher pointed to the page Pauline was to read aloud. Her skill at reading that one page was to determine her placement in a reading group. She mumbled in a low voice. When she stammered, Miss Harper filled in the word.

Pauline felt a warm blush come over her, and her hands grew cold as Miss Harper said with a sigh, “Well, you didn't fail, Pauline.” *Whew, I guess Mama's homeschoolin' paid off.*

At the end of the school day Pauline, June, Dale, and Delbert walked past row after row of houses on tree-lined streets to their temporary home on Poplar Street.

Pauline kicked at a stone, zigzagging back and forth to keep it up ahead of her, "I wanna hunt rabbits, I wanna go explorin' out on the prairie, I wanna..."

June interrupted, "Pauline, quit your complaining. You're never going to do any of those things again, so you just might as well forget it."

"Ya think ya know everything, don't ya, June? Remember what Mama always says, 'We aren't the ones in control.' Do ya remember that June? Do ya?"

Dale mumbled barely loud enough for Pauline to hear him, "I miss those things, too, Pauline."

* * * * *

One Sunday, as the family was preparing to leave for the hospital, Pauline caught sight of Daddy's harmonica. This was what she had been searching for—something to cheer Daddy up. She spit-polished it until it glistened except for a few rust spots.

At the hospital, to everyone's surprise, she timidly laid the instrument on the white sheets of Daddy's hospital bed.

As if to soothe her, Daddy held the harmonica with quivering hands and lifted the shiny, memory-filled piece to his lips. As he closed his eyes, Pauline waited for the comfort of a familiar tune. Instead, she watched in horror, as, with a limp wrist, he silently laid the harmonica back on the bed. *Is Daddy dying?* She bit her lip as she wondered how she could have been so thoughtless as to think he would want to play his harmonica when he was so deathly ill.

Mama quickly spoke up, "What a thoughtful thing to do, Pauline. It will be good for Daddy to have on hand when he feels better."

Pauline cringed as she strained to hear Daddy's voice, "Fay, I need to talk to you alone for a minute."

Mama swatted the air with her hand, causing the children to step to the other side of the wall while she pulled a wide curtain around Daddy's bed.

Pauline, June, Delbert, and Dale stood quietly in a line, ears cocked, backs against the white barricade. Pauline pressed her ear close to the curtain while staring at nothing.

June elbowed Pauline "Quit eavesdropping."

Then they heard Daddy's whispered voice, "Fay, I don't know what we're gonna do. I don't have an inkling as to how I'll make a livin' when I get outta of here."

"Jack... Jack... don't give it another thought. Look, I picked this up at the post office yesterday:

WPA

President Franklin D. Roosevelt, as part of his 'New Deal' has asked Harry L. Hopkins to oversee a Works Progress Administration Program. The WPA will hire up to 3.5 million persons making it the largest of the New Deal Projects. The WPA pays workers to labor on a variety of tasks including building fences, cleaning up and salvaging materials from abandoned farms, building roads, digging ditches, building water control structures, and constructing administration buildings.

See attached application.

The labor force of the WPA caters to middle-aged to elderly men who are without a means of supporting their families."

Mama reached for Daddy's hand. "You just relax and rest, Jack, because the good Lord and President Roosevelt will be watching over us. The doctor tells me that you'll be fit as a fiddle in no time. Here... I've already filled out the application, all you need do is sign it."

"Promise me you'll mail it tomorrow, Fay?"

"Yes, Jack. Just have faith sweetheart, okay?"

"Fay, what in the world would I do without you? I guess I never knew, until these past few months, what a rock you are."

"Don't give credit where credit's not due, Jack. It's not me..."

* * * * *

Daddy's release from the hospital made attic life seem strangely cozy. He took a job offered by the WPA, even though the doctor warned him of the risk of breathing dust of any kind.

Lying in bed one night, Pauline thought of Uncle Charlie and Aunt Julia in California. *Could a fresh start in California be the answer for us and Daddy's health?* Before drifting off to sleep, she wrote a letter in her mind.

The next morning, at the end of the school day, Pauline approached her teacher who was hunched over her desk grading assignments. "Miss Blossom, since we've been studying letter writing—ummm—I'd like to try writing a letter to my aunt in California."

"Why, Pauline, what a wonderful idea. I just happen to have a beautiful piece of stationery, an envelope, and a stamp right here in my desk. It seems, that since you are the first of my students to be so inspired, you will be the lucky recipient."

Pauline leapt down the schoolhouse steps, ignoring the heckling of the others, as she raced past them. Upon arriving at The Cousins' house, she scaled the stairs two at a time. Relieved to see that she was alone, she picked up one of Aunt Julia's letters that sat in a stack on the floor next to Mama's bedroll, searching for the return address. Kneeling on the floor, she printed her thoughts on the crisp, white paper bordered with red roses.

deer ant Julia,
i hope u are fine. is there werk for daddy?
luv Pauline

She tucked the letter under her sweater and skipped out the door to the mailbox.

* * * * *

Now that Daddy was out of the hospital, Pauline looked forward to the evenings when everyone gathered on Mama and Daddy's bed. Homework behind them, they often counted the money tucked away in a tobacco tin behind the old Victrola. Mama, invariably, thumbed through the Bible to the ribbon marking the page from the night before. It was times like these that gave Pauline an indescribable sense of peace.

Each day Pauline checked the cousin's ornate iron mailbox to no avail. Then, on one bitterly cold winter day, she reached her numb, red fingers inside and pulled out a letter addressed to 'Pauline Sampley.' After everyone was settled into bed that night, Pauline waved the envelope overhead. "I got this in the mail today!"

Smiling hopefully, she handed the unopened envelope to Mama who became momentarily speechless. With lowered eyes and a tight-lipped, puzzled smile, she inserted her forefinger under the seal, unfolded the letter, and began to read:

Dear Pauline,

The Borax Mine here in the Mojave Desert has given your Uncle a steady job with fair pay. There's a good chance your Daddy can get on too. You'll need $54.00 to make it across the border. Goes without saying, you are all welcome to keep house with us til' you can get on your feet.

Love, Aunt Julia

A long silence caused Pauline to ask herself, *Am I in trouble?*

Daddy's words interrupted, "That was a real grown-up thing to do, baby. I'm proud of you."

Pauline glanced down, fingering a torn patch on her quilt. Her skin began to feel warm—she could feel herself blushing.

Daddy avoided the penetrating eyes awaiting his reaction. "Your Mama and I will give it some thought. Now, let's git on to sleep." A murmuring of whispers followed until Daddy said, in a raised voice, "Tomorrow's a school day!"

Everyone was awake at the crack of dawn. "Your Ma and me decided that we'd best move on to Oshkosh, Wisconsin. Got wind of a farmer lookin' fer a family ta harvest beets. Comes with lodgin' too. Mama is sending a letter off to Mr. and Mrs. Yoder today. With all of us workin' we can start savin' some moolah. Then as soon as we stash away our 54 bucks, it'll be Californy 'er bust"

Late Friday afternoon, Pauline asked Mama if she could go down to the corner to wait for Daddy?"

"Goodness girl, he won't be home for another hour yet!"

"But Mama, can I, please?"

"Pauline, can't you hear that old wind howling outside? Why, you'll be frozen stiff."

"I'll dress warm, Mama."

Mama turned back to the sink shaking her head slowly. "See that you get that coat buttoned up," she hollered as Pauline slammed the door behind her.

The wind blew sharply causing tears to form in the corners of Pauline's eyes as she riveted on the distant cars coming toward her. She squinted hopefully as each one drew near. An old oak tree, too big to wrap her arms around, became her shelter from the cold.

A car slowed and pulled onto the shoulder of the road. Pauline peered from behind the tree until she saw Daddy's sweet face emerge from the back door. She ran toward him, arms open, knowing full well what to expect. Daddy lifted her off the ground as if she were as light as a tumbleweed. The driver tooted his horn as he drove away. Pauline noticed that all the men turned to look at them, with a knowing smile, when they passed.

"Runt, what are you doing out on a day like this? Why you're lucky the wind didn't jest pick ya up and blow ya away. Now, we're not excited about anything are we?"

"Daddy, do you have any news?" Pauline asked burying her head in the crevice of his neck as if that would protect her

"Well, Runt, yes, your Daddy jest happens to have a little news, and I will share it with the whole family at the supper table tonight." He smiled and winked at her saying, "Come on, I'll race ya home."

Pauline ran hard and fast next to Daddy as he took long, slow strides. Nearing the door, Pauline pulled ahead of him squealing, "I beat, I beat."

"Yes, you beat me, but look what I had to carry," said Daddy, holding out his black lunch bucket. Their laughter spilled over into the kitchen where Mama walked toward them balancing a bowl of beans in one hand and a plate of biscuits in the other.

"Well, I see you found your Daddy." Mama held her arms wide apart while waiting for Daddy's kiss on the cheek. Barely missing a step she called out, "Time for supper everyone, get washed up."

Over supper, Daddy seemed to delight in keeping the family waiting in suspense. Finally, he spoke, "We leave fer Oshkosh, Wisconsin, in eight weeks." The family leaned forward in their chairs, all eyes and ears, until Daddy finished. "We'll be livin' and workin' on a beet farm. We'll tend the soil, plant and harvest the beets, and do anything that needs doin' 'round the farm. By the time Ol' Man Winter rears his ugly head again, we'll have our $54 and be on our way to sunny California."

Mama and the children looked on in disbelief, each engrossed in their own thoughts. Then, Daddy was suddenly flooded with questions.

"Where will we live in Oshkosh?"

"Will we have to go to school?"

"Will there be other farm workers there?"

"Whoa, I ain't got all the answers! Let's jest be thankful fer the job."

* * * * *

As the Oakland pulled away, Mama blotted her eyes with her hankie. Everyone waved at the two sisters, who stood wrapped in each other's arms until they seemed like miniature silhouettes against their white frame house with its green roof and shutters.

Mama spoke tearfully, trying to divert everyone's attention, "Kids, just last week I heard on the radio that President Roosevelt has published his first book about the New Deal. It's titled, *Looking Forward*, and that's just what we Sampleys are doing, looking forward."

Chapter Six

It was early spring of 1936. The wind pushed hard against each curve and crevice of the car. A piercing whistle screamed through every little cranny.

Pauline's cheek vibrated while pressed against the moist window cooled by the early spring air. She stretched her dull red sweater down over her knees—stressing the frayed shoulder seams. She rubbed at the goose bumps that had formed between the top of her socks and hem of her dress, hoping the friction would warm the exposed part of her legs. Shivering, she tugged at one of Mama's neatly folded quilts, slipping her legs into one of the warm deep folds. Trying hard to imagine what awaited them in Oshkosh she closed her eyes tightly. Her strawberry blonde lashes flickered as her imagination raced with visions of days to come.

Pauline's thoughts were interrupted by her siblings rousting about on the backseat bed that Mama put together the night before. Pots, pans, and other odds and ends rattled underneath a pile of once-carefully-folded quilts. The wrestling, tickling and giggling soon faded into bickering, pinching, and tattling. Daddy went into a coughing fit, which made Mama turn to them with a heavy sigh "All of you lie down and close your eyes now!"

Grumbling, the four tried to fit themselves together like tight pieces of a puzzle. Delbert's long-awaited growth spurt made him the target of shoving and loud whispering. "Get on your own side, ya hog." All the while keeping a close eye on the back of Mama's head.

At first, the sound of rope beating against the side of the car and the mattress heaving up and down on the roof had fought off sleep for Pauline. After a while though, she became absorbed in the harsh musical rhythm. She closed her eyes to recall Uncle John, in his bib overalls, one foot propped up on the edge of a large metal washtub. In her mind, his head bobbled as he strummed the tight cord that was strung from the top of a broom handle down to the center of the tub. She pictured Aunt Julia, precariously perched on the edge of a crate, legs spread, toes tapping, as she loosely held two spoons pressed back to back between her pointer and middle finger. She slapped them rhythmically against her weighty thigh to the tune of "Ain't She Sweet." The imaginary dull strumming of a washtub bass and sharp clatter of spoons along with the heavy breathing and snoring of the others eventually lulled her into a deep, drooling sleep.

* * * * *

Pauline, June, Dale, and Delbert stirred restlessly for a long while before poking their tangled heads up from their slipshod habitat. Two at each window, they all stared dumbfounded at the continuous sight of rolling green hills dotted with woodlands of chartreuse trees. A winding, gushing river, swollen from the winter's melted snow, rapidly gouged its path through the contour of the hills.

It had been a long trip to Wisconsin, but finally, the car slowed to cross a makeshift bridge over a narrow creek and pulled up in front of a two-story farmhouse. Daddy had no sooner turned off the engine than a silver-haired couple appeared on the front porch. They walked to Daddy's side of the car, where the man introduced himself as Mr. Yoder and his wife, Mrs. Ester Yoder. The portly woman smiled, squeezing her eyes into narrow slits while her husband clamped his lips together tightly — eyes darting to and fro warily.

Everyone piled out of the car adjusting their clothes and stretching arms and legs in all directions.

Mr. Yoder got right to business. He extended his arms, pointing out toward a never-ending field of chunky black soil. Lifting his machete out of its holster, he held up an invisible bunch of beets — slicing the air with the sharp, shiny blade. He yelled, "Whack, and it's done!"

Pauline swallowed hard.

Mr. Yoder turned and flashed a serious gaze toward the sky as if searching for the right words, "I expect you to prepare the soil, plant, and harvest." Pauline listened intently. "Ester here will bring you sandwiches and drinks at noon each work day. The nearest town for groceries and other supplies is twenty miles away. We expect eight hours, six days a week." Pauline held her breath during a moment of silence before he spoke again while staring down at the ground, "We'll show you to your lodging now, but... I'd better say beforehand that we regret we can't do better."

They followed Mr. Yoder's rusty, red pickup-truck to a grassy hilltop. Their eyes rested on a desolate cabin that looked as if it could be easily threatened by a good windstorm. Pauline noticed

Mama's eyes widen and her head drop. She wondered if the beat of Mama's heart could be seen through her faded, yellow dress.

As they made their way up the hill, the sweet unfamiliar fragrance of fresh green grass tempted the children to stretch out horizontally and roll down—arms high above their heads. Their rolling and squealing carried on for quite a while before they began to wonder where Mama and Daddy were.

Nearing the cabin, they hesitated as they overheard Mama and Daddy speaking in low voices. Pauline followed June as the four quietly crossed the threshold to discover their parents with arms wrapped around each other—as if drawing strength from one another. They were encircled by streaks of light shining through cracks in the roof and sidewalls.

Mama let her hands fall to her side while turning to her puzzled, disheveled youngsters. "We sure have a lot to be thankful for, don't we kids? Beautiful country, good hard work to do, and just being able to stay together. You know, many children had to be farmed out to other relatives during these hard times. Poor souls must be grief stricken."

Daddy had been listening halfheartedly while scanning the land. "With a little luck, that windmill ya see over there will give us water right to the house."

Pauline recognized the symptoms. *He's tryin' to make the best of things. Tryin' to cheer Mama up and help her see what this place could be.*

"Next Saturday we'll go to town for supplies and talk to Mr. Yoder 'bout that scrap lumber he mentioned. Then, later in the week, the boys and I will work on the outside of the cabin— patchin' and fillin' cracks. Fay, you and the girls will have the inside lookin' like home in no time."

Pauline wondered why girls were always expected to scrub and clean instead of doing something fun, like carrying wood and hitting nails, but she convinced herself that this wasn't the time to ask such questions.

The next morning everyone donned their work clothes and set about their chores. Daddy and the boys began preparing the fields for planting, and Mama and the girls took the washboard down to the creek along with a bar of soap. After the laundry was all scrubbed and rinsed, Pauline and June spread the clothes out on branches in the sun to dry.

* * * * *

During breakfast on Saturday morning, Mama looked as if she would burst as she pushed her chair back, walked over to Pauline and kissed her on the forehead.

"What's that for?" Asked Pauline.

"Happy birthday, honey!"

"Today's my birthday?"

Daddy's eyes twinkled and his lips spread into a tight smile. "Yep, you're growing up sweetheart; you're growing up."

Mama had a bucket of creek water heating on the wood stove. Her heavy black flat iron sat face down, hot, and ready to press the worst of the wrinkles out of their stiff, sun-dried clothes. Each of the four youngsters took their turn bathing in the rough, metal, tub, starting with the eldest to the youngest.

On the way to town that afternoon, Pauline closed her eyes shivering at the harsh odor of lye reeking from everyone's skin and hair. Heads were rotating from side-to-side in unison, as they took in the sights of their new territory.

The clan scanned Main Street, spotting a grocery and hardware store. Daddy parked the Oakland diagonally in front of a sign that read "Herb's Hardware" Two prickly faced men sat crouched on a bench outside, cigarettes dangling from deeply creased lips— eyelids drooping.

Pauline watched longingly as Daddy and the boys took long strides toward an off-kilter screen door set well under the roof. A cowbell, somewhere on the door, alerted the clerk of their entry.

Pauline followed Mama and June, arms folded, pouting in defiance about the hardware store expedition she was missing out on—until the faint sound of music distracted her.

Mama and the girls slowed their pace and gawked through the store window where a radio in a fine wooden cabinet stood on display. Pauline and June begged, "Oh, Mama, could we please go in... just for a few minutes?"

"Well, I can't see any reason why not? It's Saturday, and it's Pauline's birthday."

They gazed at each other in disbelief when they realized that the spirited, twangy song drifting through the cloth covered radio speakers was about them.

"Folks are actually writing songs about the trouble we've seen," said Mama.

Pauline laughed "Old Man Depression sure done us wrong, didn't he, Mama?"

"There's a reason for everything, Pauline... a reason for everything." The lyrics to the song "Dust Bowl Refugee" flooded the air.

Once they were in the grocery store, Pauline and June carried baskets for Mama, filling them with sugar, flour, coffee, salt, beans, yeast, lard, eggs, milk, and cornmeal. They walked stiff-legged, using their knees for support as their baskets became heavier and heavier. Lagging behind, they rounded a corner to see Mama staring wistfully at a colorful display of flower seeds. Pauline and June set their baskets down at the foot of the stand that Mama was turning slowly—pondering. The three seemed lost in their own world. Pauline and June began organizing handfuls of their favorite flower packets like a hand of cards.

"Oh, Mama, can we buy one?" Asked Pauline.

Mama rubbed a dry, cracked, hand over her forehead and half closed eyes. She pinched the bridge of her nose between her thumb and forefinger holding the pose tightly. "Well, Pauline, since it's your birthday, you may choose one packet."

Pauline immediately cut her eyes toward June who had already folded her arms high across her chest.

June whined, "But, Mama, I didn't get anything on my birthday!"

"June, we couldn't afford anything on your birthday. This is something we can give Pauline that will be pleasing to the whole family."

"You're right, Mama. I shouldn't be so selfish. Which one will you choose, Pauline?"

"Which do you like, June, the sweet peas or forget-me-nots?"

"Come on Pauline. You pick. After all, it's your birthday."

"Girls, we have lollygagged long enough. Daddy and the boys will be wondering where in heaven's name we are."

"I'll choose the sweet peas," said Pauline.

Mama nudged them toward the cash register. The clerk looked them over. "Why what brought you folks to town? Oh, you're the Yoder's new hired hands. Everyone's been a wonderin' who he'd get this year? Last year they hired a family of eight. The mister fell on his machete and crippled himself—most likely for life. Wife and kids tried to keep up with the work, but she wore down quick, and most of the kids were too young to be of much use. Yoders had to let them go. Pitiful. It was just 'fore harvest, and the Yoders worked day and night. Yep, the whole town was worried 'bout em, at their age an' all."

Pauline waved as she spotted Daddy coming out of the hardware store. She darted across the street throwing her arms around him. "Look what Mama bought me for my birthday, Daddy—sweet peas."

"Well, Pauline, if that don't beat all, your first birthday gift! Happy birthday, Runt."

On the way home Daddy's face grew serious. "Our first day of work as a family is just around the corner. Tomorrow afternoon, the boys and I will meet with Mr. Yoder to talk 'bout the plan he has for us—ta get a feel for things. This time it'll be all up to us, yes sir, just us Sampleys showin' what we're made of."

Mama chimed in, "And while you and the boys are getting filled in, the girls and I can begin repairing the roof."

"Oh no, you won't! It'll be a cold day in hell when I see you and my girls up on a roof. That's a job for the men of the family. Just be patient, Fay. We'll get to it in a day or so."

Mama looked as if she was already thinking about something else.

"Did ya hear me, Fay?"

"Oh...uh...huh...yes, Jack, I hear you."

Sunday morning after Daddy and the boys started down the lane, Pauline noticed Mama standing in the doorway—shovel in hand. "Ma, what are ya doin' with that shovel?"

Mama seemed deep in thought. "You and June will need to work as a team to get that sod up on the roof to me. So, wake June up and get dressed. Time's a wasting."

"But Mama Daddy said..."

"Oh, Pauline, your Daddy was just being protective."

Mama stomped the ground hard with her heel searching for just the right combination of grassy sod. Then she slipped the shovel under a plot of the moist roof patch, lifting it onto June and Pauline's outstretched arms. Together they strained awkwardly as they placed each section around the footing of the cabin—just as Mama instructed.

Mama wiped the sweat from her forehead with the back of her sleeve. "Now, that may be just enough," she said as she peered over her shoulder toward the Yoder's farm.

As the three stood gazing toward the roof, arms limp; Mama explained her plan, step-by-step. "I'll get up on the roof. Pauline, you will hand the sod patches to June who will be standing on top of those two wood boxes. Then June will pass them up to me. Simple as that."

June eyeballed the two rickety boxes. "Guess this is what Daddy meant by 'a cold day in hell,'" she whispered.

"Ah, June, ya chicken liver. I'll get up there... ya want me to get up there?"

"No, Pauline, you are way too young."

Mama appeared unaware of the ruckus going on around her, as

she talked to herself and anyone else interested in listening. "I will fill in all of the crevices, and the grass will keep right on growing. The roots will drink up the rain, keeping us nice and dry. It will be just like our soddy out in the Panhandle."

June hollered up to Mama who was crawling across the roof on her hands and knees. "Ma, we didn't have any rain when we lived in Texas."

"Come on girls, no more dillydallying. We don't have forever—you know. Let's sing while we work. Singing always makes work seem less like work. 'Amaaaaazing Grace, how sweet the sound...'"

Pauline sensed something in her soul that day, a kind of rebellious delight, until a rumbling on the roof interrupted the harmony of their song. Their joy faded to fear when a shrill scream was heard from somewhere overhead followed by a leg dangling off the edge of the roof. Pauline and June scrambled to steady Mama as her toes tapped the air while desperately trying to find something solid to stand on. While frantically trying to place Mama's foot on top of the two crates, the corner of Pauline's eye noticed the Oakland rounding the bend.

"Ma, here they come! Daddy will be mad as a hornet!"

Mama brushed herself off as she caught her breath, "Oh honey, I really don't think so. I think he'll be proud that we took on the task—saving him some work."

Daddy's stride was purposeful as he shaded his eyes with the flat of his hand to better view their undertaking. "Fay, what the heck were you doing up there?"

Pauline wanted to hide but decided it would be better to face Daddy's wrath, so she stood petrified, breathless.

"I wanted to surprise you, Jack."

Pauline and June rolled their eyes toward Mama and flinched when Daddy flung both hands toward the sky. "Fay, if you don't beat all! Come on boys, we might as well give them a hand," he said, shaking his head and grinning at the ground. "Lord, give me strength."

Chapter Seven

The beet tops were a rich, reddish green, a good sign according to Mr. Yoder.

The Sampleys stood in the middle of a musty smelling, storage barn. Each member of the family was handed a machete. It was harvest time.

Mr. Yoder grasped a bunch of beets in his left hand, and while suspending the cluster at arm's length; he raised his machete and chopped the tops off precisely where they connected to their offspring. The beets toppled into a bushel basket waiting on the uneven dirt floor of the barn. "That's all there is to it," he said with a tight-lipped grin. "Are ya ready to give 'er a go?"

* * * * *

The weighty blade seemed to grow heavier as the day wore on. No one complained. Pauline was thankful just to be there, instead of in a stuffy 'ol classroom somewhere.

Mrs. Yoder, approaching with lunch that day, was a welcome sight.

The Sampleys sat under a raggedy weeping willow tree near the west end of the front yard. The spindly branches, catching the slightest hint of a breeze, danced gracefully.

By Friday afternoon, Pauline's right wrist and arm had become weak, puffy and feverish to the touch. She could see Dale just two rows over, his hair wet with sweat and face flushed. He had taken to laying bunches of beets on the ground and swinging his machete with both hands to sever the tops off. He twisted hard at the waist to take some of the weight off of his shoulders. Fear crept over her. *What if we aren't strong enough? What if we can't do it? What about California then?*

In the early evening, Pauline discreetly suggested that Dale join her at the creek. "Dale, look for a stick so we can stir this mud into a thick paste."

"Why?"

"Just do it, Dale. I heard tell that great grandpa once saved Daddy's life when he was snake bit, most likely a rattler. Yep, said he packed a fist full of thick, gooey, mud from the creek bottom on it. Left it there till it dried and fell off. After that, he was good as new. Said it takes the swelling down, draws the poison and soreness out. Daddy says it's better than anythin' an ol' doc would give ya."

"But, Pauline, Mama always makes a paste of baking soda and water. Remember, she calls it a poultice?"

"I knooowww Dale, but we don't want Mama knowin' that we're a sufferin', now do we? You know how she gets. So, we ain't gonna go complainin' to Ma, ya hear?"

"Yep, I hear, Pauline."

After supper, June dangled both wrists painfully over the

washbasin. "My wrists are too sore to lift one more dish." Pauline shot a quick glance toward Dale as if he were asking permission to chime in. Lips taut, Pauline ignored his plea as she stared off into space.

Without looking up, Mama said, "All I can tell you, June, is to soak your wrists in cold creek water, then pack them with mud to draw the soreness out."

Dale and Pauline stood motionless—eyebrows arched high. June must have felt Mama's sense of helplessness because her eyes suddenly fixed on the floor as if she had lost something.

*****

Later that night Mama sat her Treasure Chest on her lap and lifted the lid. June and Pauline ran to her side to see if great grandmother's Lavaliere was still intact. Mama had promised both girls that they would be allowed to wear the fragile necklace at their high school graduations and on their wedding days. She dangled it from her fingertips, reminding the girls again. "This is the only thing I have of my Mother's—I wore it when I graduated from high school."

That's the only good reason I can think of to go to school, thought Pauline.

Then Mama lifted the Bible out of the bottom of the box. The pages were dog-eared, and the gold lettering was nearly worn off its leather cover. Mama carefully ran her red, swollen fingers across the recessed lettering on cracked leather cover. She then ran one finger on the page where a faded purple ribbon lay. She read, 1 Corinthians 4:11,12. *Even unto this present hour we both hunger, and thirst, and are naked, and are buffeted, and have no certain dwelling place; And labor, working with our own hands; being reviled, we bless; being persecuted, we suffer it.*"

* * * * *

The weekly get-togethers with aunts, uncles, and cousins were sorrowfully missed. As fate would have it though, the Yoders, or at least Mrs. Yoder, started a tradition of inviting the Sampleys to Sunday supper.

On one such Sunday Pauline thought, *There is always a poignant scent in the air here, probably, from the bunches of Queen Anne's lace, asters, and daisies posing in oddly shaped vases, and sitting on top of dollies placed on the kitchen table, or in a sunny window. I know Mama loves that.*

Pauline marveled at Mrs. Yoder's small feet scurrying around the kitchen. *She's sort of pretty for an older person with her long silver hair pulled up in a bun, and damp wispy curls loose here and there. Her dress isn't faded like Mama's, and Mama doesn't serve meals on white plates with gold trim. I bet she will someday though.*

Sitting at the table, Pauline's eyes rested on Mr. Yoder. *He is nothing like Daddy. His voice is gruff—kinda mean soundin'. Can't help but wonder if he jest thinks of us as poor Okies and only allows us to come to Sunday dinner out of the goodness of his wife's heart. Was right good lumber he gave us though. Would have been tough gettin' along without any shelves in the cabin. Guess he isn't so bad after all. Kinda strange the way Mama insisted that June and I never go into his barn alone? Jest didn't seem like somethin' she'd say.*

Pauline eyed Mr. Yoder's red suspenders. His belly bulged between the wide, elastic straps, making it resemble a rain barrel stashed directly under the double chin that jiggled each time he found cause to speak.

It was after one of these Sunday dinners that Mr. Yoder nonchalantly mentioned, "While I was working in the tractor barn yesterday, I discovered an old Victrola. Prob'bly don't work, but if you folks want to try fixin' it, it's yers. Come on out to the barn and I'll show ya."

Pauline started to leap off her chair before she remembered Mama's warning about going to the barn alone with Mr. Yoder crossed her mind. It had puzzled her at the time, but Mama's eyes were a dark, deep blue when she said it. She settled back into her chair until Daddy and the boys got up, then followed them across the front porch and down the lane to the barn.

"Well, here it is. You may be able to fix 'er up? Guess there ain't much that can go wrong with a Victrola?. I only found one record."

He squinted to read the title, "Oh it's "Shine on Harvest Moon." You know it, don't cha?"

Daddy and Delbert loaded the dusty old Victrola onto the backseat of the Oakland.

* * * * *

Sitting in the middle of the cabin floor, Pauline stripped off her socks using one to wipe the dust from the metal, cone-shaped speaker that resembled a large, trumpet-shaped morning glory flower. "Look, Daddy, it still has some of the gold lettering. Oh no... the hand crank is frozen solid from rust."

She pounded the handle with her fist, until Daddy, bending down to her level, broke her frustrated anger. "Pauline, never force anything. That only makes things worse."

Wincing, she turned away. "Daddy, you'll never know how much I've longed for real music in my life. Um… not that I don't like your music Daddy, but at my age, a girl can learn a lot 'bout what's goin' on in the world from the words of a song. Course I don't mean 'bout love and boys and such, but jest 'bout what other folks like us is a-doin' and a-thinkin'. Ya know what I mean, Daddy?"

"Yeah, Runt, I guess I do know what ya mean. I guess I know my girl is a-growin' up too. Now get me 'bout a teaspoon of Mama's lard. We'll rub us a little on that ol' rust and just ease 'er back and forth 'til she breaks loose."

Delbert chuckled, poking Daddy in the ribs. "Hey, you crank that ol' Victrola the same way you crank the Oakland, 'cept without the kickin' and cussin'."

"Delbert, you're in the presence of ladies," muttered Daddy.

"Those aren't ladies… those are my sisters."

Daddy rolled his eyes. "Give me the record, Pauline."

"Here Daddy. I cleaned it off real good with my sock."

Mama, sitting at her sewing machine, glowered. "Pauline, if it kills me, I am going to insist that you improve your grammar and begin speaking like an educated young woman. 'I cleaned it real good' is definitely not good English. Daddy's right… you are growing up, and it's time you begin to act like it."

"Please, not now Mama, I can't think 'bout nothing' 'cept hearin' that record."

Mama lifted both hands toward the sky, "Lord, give me strength."

Daddy placed the small hole in the center of the black disc-shaped record over the thin metal spindle. Then he grabbed the handle on the side of the wooden cabinet and gave it a good crank. Once the record began to spin, he eyeballed the placement of the arm holding the needle, making sure the sharp point met with the smooth edge of the record—just ahead of the grooves where the music itself was embedded.

As the music leaked through the cracked, chinking between the log walls, Pauline wondered how strange the scratchy melody must sound to the animals crouched low in the darkness outside.

> *…shine on*
> *Shine on harvest moon*
> *Up in the sky*
> *I ain't had no lovin' since January, February, June or July*

* * * * *

After chores, Pauline and Dale grabbed their fishing poles from a cavity in the old oak tree near the south side of the house. Pauline's story about how they came to shelter their poles inside a tree was familiar, yet Dale still hung on every word.

"See here, Dale. It's still black where a bolt of lightning must have leaped right out of the sky and nearly split this tree trunk in half. It's a wonder she's still a standin'. Aren't you glad we weren't livin' here way back then? I s'pose her bark has been tryin' to heal her deep wound for ages? Yep, it's only by the grace of God that she lived through it." Once again Dale, mouth agape, rubbed the tips of his fingers down the jagged black streak.

"Let's go fishin', Pauline."

The two stood knee-deep in the creek, lost in their search for a stray fish or two.

"Dale, do you remember the day we rigged our fishing poles?"

Dale rolled his eyes. "Oh yeah, I'll never forget it."

"Me neither... never felt so guilty in all my life. Remember how things just kinda snuck up on us? We found nice straight sticks, but then just looked at each other; a-wonderin' where in the world we'd get lines and hooks. Remember I stole two needles and a spool of thread when Ma wasn't looking? Don't know what came over me. I'll regret it for the rest of my life. Wonder why Mama never said anything?"

The only excitement of the day was the sight of worms twisting and turning on Mama's bent sewing needle. *Prob'bly our punishment for stealin' from Mama?*

"Come on, Dale, looks like all we're gonna catch is a cold."

Pauline had grown to anticipate the result of her dry sense of humor; predictably, no matter how many times Dale heard her one-liners, he nearly fell down laughing. An ample pair of lips normally hid Dale's patchwork of teeth. But, when he broke out in uncontrollable laughter, the sight of his one oversized tooth next to its odd partner, a squared off smattering of a tooth surrounded by a puffy ring of red gum tissue—made his laughter contagious.

* * * * *

Pauline and Dale amused themselves by making bird traps. The trigger on the wooden box was so sensitive that even a pair of boots jarring the ground would set it off. Unlike fishing, the plan—perfected by practice, was a sure thing.

Pauline and Dale stretched out flat on their stomachs behind the woodpile, not allowing their breath to stir even a blade of grass. Pauline, since she was the eldest, wrapped the string around her forefinger with the other end tied to a slender twig propping up one side of the box. Next, focusing one eye through a crevice in the log pile, she and Dale waited until the cautious victim was enticed under the box by the tempting sight of worms and berries. Once it reached dead center, she snapped the string as if snagging a fish. Then they took turns peering through a knothole on top of the box for a close-up look at their captured prey. After getting their fill, they flipped the box over and lay on their backs waiting for the creature to realize its freedom and fly away into the clouds.

Chapter Eight

Pauline felt terrible guilt pains when she climbed the windmill tower — as Mama and Daddy had strictly forbidden it. She prayed about the temptation to no avail, knowing full well that it was a devious sin of the worst kind.

Why do I do it? Even waiting until their car goes down the lane to the Yoder's and making sure June is well engrossed in one of her books? 'Course, Dale isn't a problem... shoot, he begs to do it too! I hate makin' him stay on the ground, but it would be way too dangerous for him.

Leastways, I only do it when the pump is shut down. Wouldn't take the risk of gettin' knocked to the ground with one of those blades— flattened like a buckwheat pancake.

I'm lucky I have so much to snitch on Dale—that—he'd never dare tattle on me. Delbert just hollers, "Dad-burn you Pauline, get the hell down from there!" 'Course, he'd only say "hell" when Mama and Daddy aren't around. It is worth it to have to do his chores for a whole week just to keep him from tellin'?

I simply couldn't bear it if Daddy found out I did somethin' behind their backs. Yet up on that platform, I can see for miles. I can see clear to the edge of town, and I can see when Mama and Daddy head home from the Yoder's.

As an added precaution, cupping her hands around her mouth, she hollered down at Dale, who sat pouting with his knees tucked under his chin. "Dale, if you don't tell, I'll take you to the creek tomorrow."

He perked up, and cupping his hands around his mouth, hollered back up, "Okaaay."

* * * * *

Late the next afternoon Mama, Pauline, and Dale, walked home from the field after finishing their work early. Pauline ran up ahead to catch up with Dale. "Hey, ya wanna go to the creek when we get home?"

"Ah, Pauline, ya remembered."

"Yep, I'm jest like Daddy that-away. I always keep my word."

The two sat on a boulder, dangling their bare feet in the calmly flowing creek. Dale looked over at Pauline, his eyes large and bright. "So, whatcha wanna do, Pauline?"

"I've been a rackin' my brain, Dale, and I think we should study."

"Study? Are ya feelin' alright, Pauline? Study what?"

"Study frog life. It won't be easy 'cause we'll have ta haul rocks, and they'll have ta fit together jest so. We'll make us a frog pen. It'll be on the shore. We can't take them away from what they're used to... why, they'd jest die. We'll have to figure out a way to keep them from jumping out, too. It'll be kinda like our bird traps... we'll study them... then we'll set them free."

"Pauline, what about weaving some sticks in between the rocks, maybe that'll keep them in?"

"Might be worth a try, Dale. If not, I'm sure an idea will come to us once we set our minds to it."

Hours passed before the last stone was in place and the sought after frogs were within the boundaries of their pen. Pauline and Dale, covered with mud, lay down in the creek, clothes and all. Hands pushing against the rocky bed, they allowed their legs to float freely in the current. Swishing from side to side, Pauline's dress reminded her of fins. She smiled a satisfied smile.

Pauline and Dale wrung their clothes tightly until it felt as if their skin would be pinched in the knot. Tying shoelaces together, they each draped their shoes over one shoulder and started up a deer trail to the house. Taking the lead, winding her way past bushes and saplings threatening to overtake the path, Pauline uttered in a matter-of-fact way, "I'm as hungry as a bear comin' out of hibernation."

"Ah, Pauline, how in the heck would ya know anything 'bout bears, you ain't never even seen one?"

"Um... maybe... maybe not? Ya know... there are bears right here in the woodlands of Oshkosh, don't ya?"

"Naw, you're full of baloney."

"There are all kinda wild animals here in Oshkosh—killer bears, mountain lions, rattlers, vampire bats. Yep, its mighty dangerous country we're a-livin' in."

Noticing Dale's Adam's apple bobbing up and down, and his right eye beginning to twitch, Pauline straightened her shoulders and lifted her knees higher, marching the rest of the way home in silence.

Emerging from the woods, the glow of the sunset shone on Pauline's face, bringing about the familiar stinging of another dreaded sunburn. *I hope Mama won't be cross with me for forgetting my bonnet. If she is, it will ruin everything.*

Pauline headed toward the supper table, trying to avoid the once over from Mama. She nudged Dale. "Hey, whatcha doin', Pauline, don't be shoving me around!" Then he seemed to realize that they would be better off causing as little commotion as possible. He quietly shuffled along behind his sister.

*****

Before daylight the next morning, Pauline awakened to the sound of thunder and raindrops dripping through the roof and bouncing off the wood floor like pellets from a Red Rider BB Gun. So much for our sod roof, she thought.

"Pssst... Dale, wake up. The creek must have turned into raging rapids by now. Its prob'bly flowed over the bank."

Pauline glanced at Dale who leaped out of his bed, tears forming in the corners of his eyes. "Pauline, we gotta go, we gotta save em. What if they're trapped and can't get out? We can't let em die, jest cause you wanted to do a stupid ol' study."

Pauline inched away from the soaked corner of her bedroll. "Dale, the frogs are gone... doin' what God created them to do. That dad-burned flimsy, frog pen we made ain't no way gonna hold up to the current of a creek swollen from the rain. The frogs are free now—jest like our birds, huh, Dale? It's the way it's s'ppose to be."

Pauline turned her back on Dale and walked away—shoulders slumped and head hanging.

Despite Dale's sniveling, Pauline overheard a faint, "Sorry, Pauline."

* * * * *

Perhaps the forewarning should have been the angry, tumbling, black and gray clouds that gave the fields a mystical look on that dreadful day.

Only the sound of machete's snapping off beet stems broke the silence of the bent over troop; when Delbert let loose a nightmarish shriek.

Heavily clotted rows of earth seemed like barriers separating the family from Delbert. They stumbled across the rows with arms flailing, Pauline, and Dale, the first to arrive seemed frozen in time as they gawked at the gaping gash revealing the bone of Delbert's profusely bleeding finger. It was Daddy who broke the spell.

He quickly pulled off his shirt and applied pressure on the wound, attempting to reunite the two pieces of dangling flesh. Then Daddy and Delbert took nearly identical strides as, arm in arm, they headed toward the Yoder's house, leaving a trail of blood behind them.

Mrs. Yoder must have seen the troop crossing the field as if announced by the thunder that rumbled all around them. Pauline looked up at the sky. *Please God, not now.* Mrs. Yoder held the door open, her face aged with concern. Noticing the blood-soaked cloth covering Delbert's finger she sprang into action, responding to each of Daddy's requests.

"I need clean, white cloth, boiled water, a needle, thread and some whiskey."

"I have all of that," she said as she carried a kettle of water to the stove while bent on controlling her trembling hands.

Daddy motioned for everyone to hold Delbert down as he dowsed his open wound with the whiskey. Delbert's face distorted. He howled like a wounded animal. Huge beads of perspiration broke out on his forehead as he clenched his teeth together hard. Daddy stitched his finger together with the grace of a seamstress. He then wrapped it with strips of clean white cloth

Mrs. Yoder expelled a sigh of relief while stating firmly, "I think you all need to take the rest of the day off." Pauline's mouth dropped open. *Is she an angel who fell from heaven?*

The slamming of the back door seemed to echo off the walls of the small kitchen. Mr. Yoder stood tall, peering down at the bloody mess. "Appears there's been an accident. I'm sorry about that, but there will be no days off. Ester, you know we're on a schedule. I'll drive Delbert home, and the rest of you can get back to work."

Anger swept over Pauline as the family watched Mr. Yoder drive off with Delbert. *I hate Mr. Yoder. Daddy is the head of this family. I hate the way Mama and Daddy look now—shoulders drooping—heads hanging.* She trailed behind the rest as they made their way back to the fields. *I wish I hadn't teased Delbert 'bout growing whiskers this morning.*

As if Daddy were reading Pauline's mind, he stopped at the edge of the field to put his arm around Mama's shoulders, then spoke in a voice loud enough for the rest to hear. "Don't worry. I fixed him up real good. He'll be fit as a fiddle in no time."

✼ ✼ ✼ ✼ ✼

Summer passed quickly, and the winding down of harvest season found the Sampley's spending long nights around the kitchen table doing schoolwork. Pauline had rejoiced at the thought of no school for a year, but had hoped that meant no school at all. Whining and complaining were useless, and only seemed to make Mama more strong-willed.

Each night, before Bible and bed, Daddy played his harmonica with the unspoken expectation that the others would join in somehow. The clan drank in the soulful sounds until they could no longer help themselves and were compelled to sing along, attempting to harmonize or accompany Daddy by clicking the backs of two spoons together, or stroking Mama's washboard.

Weekly, Daddy assigned someone the enviable task of counting the savings. Often, this was a time for sharing California dreams. Daddy wished for a job with a regular paycheck. Mama wished for a home with a big front porch, and a flower and vegetable garden. June wished to live near a library and graduate from high school.

Pauline wished that the family would always be together. At this, Daddy reached over and patted her leg. Then she rather reluctantly added, "And I wanna graduate from high school, too, so I can wear the Lavaliere." Dale wished for a brand new pair of boy's shoes. The room filled with contagious laughter that came to an abrupt halt when Delbert shared his wish. "I dream of joining the Civilian Conservation Corps. I heard about it from some of the fellas at school."

From the look of dismay on the faces of Pauline, June, and Dale, he might just as well have said he was planning to jump over the Grand Canyon. An uncomfortable silence filled the room.

Pauline counted the bills and the change under a huddle of

peering eyes. "Fifty-Two, Fifty-Three, and Fifty-Four." *Yes, it was enough. It was enough!*

With hesitation, she asked what had been praying on her mind since Delbert first spoke of it, "What the devil is Civilian Conservation Corps?"

Pauline barely got the words out of her mouth when Mama replied, "Its often called CCC. It's a project President Roosevelt created for taking care of the people and the land. It gives boys between the ages of 17 and 28 a chance to work so they can send money home. They plant trees, fight fires, build dams, and maintain and improve the national parks.

The thought of Pauline's hot-tempered, red-faced brother fighting fires seemed to paralyze her. She heard the rest of Mama's definition through a fog of racing thoughts.

Obviously ignoring Delbert's dream, Mama continued, "Yes, Pauline, the President saw the farmers greedily stripping the land, leaving nothing but a dust bowl behind. He saw people going hungry. It's a practical solution! Just like your Daddy said—we can't just take from the land—we need to give back too."

Daddy's eyes welled up with tears. "You're very bright, son. You figured out what your Ma and I knew all along—until we get settled it's going to be darn tight survivin' in California. Your dream is a good dream, son.

Delbert's voice sounded a couple of octaves deeper that usual. "Sampleys, I not only want to join the CCC—I need to join. I'll be able to save $25 a month. We all know that money could either make or break us."

Delbert gave a quick glance toward Mama, who now sat with her head down and shoulders drooping. He gently walked to her side, pulling her close. "Now, Mama, it's only for six months and then we'll all be together again out in Californy. Now that the end of harvest season is in sight, you and Daddy can just drop me off at an enlistment site. Gotta be one somewhars nearby." Mama didn't say a word.

In the quiet before bedtime, Mama read the Bible to her ragdoll family who seemed cleansed by the ambiance of the night. Jeremiah 29:11. *For I know the thoughts that I think toward you, saith the Lord, thoughts of peace, and not of evil, to give you an expected end."*

Morning found the Sampley's saying a tearful goodbye while hugging Mrs. Yoder and dutifully shaking hands with Mr. Yoder. Accompanied by Mama's prayers, they were on their way to California. The beet fields were nothing but a black sea now, dotted with caps of white snow.

Chapter Nine

Pauline remembered a cold Wisconsin night—sitting on Daddy's knee as he carefully unfolded a crisp, dog-eared map, piecing together the torn folds. He held Pauline's spindly finger in his rough, dry hand, and together they traced the squiggly black line from Wisconsin to California. They swayed slightly back and forth as if dancing a slow dance, as Daddy exaggerated each curve in the road.

* * * * *

Delbert's enthusiasm, and the fact that his CCC stint would only be six months, made dropping him off at the enlistment office more bearable. Before they turned to leave, Mama stuffed Uncle Charlie and Aunt Julia's address into the palm of his hand.

Pauline hummed to the beat of tires bouncing off stones and cracks in the pavement. Mouth agape, lips protruding, she strained to create an unpredictable melody, at best. She held each note until face red and cheeks puffed, she gasped for another breath.

Pauline tilted her head back against the threadbare, musty-smelling upholstery. She inhaled the surprising scent of Grandma's attic trunk. *But I was only four or five years old when I last saw my Grandma.* Through half closed eyes Pauline saw Mama frowning at her, brows cocked hopefully. "Pauline, why don't you take a nap?"

"But Mama, I'm not a bit tired." She resumed her humming as if not wanting to lose track of where she left off, oblivious to the sight of Mama's body limply retreating.

The rhythm created by the uneven pavement gently tugged at Pauline's reddish-blonde eyelashes. Pale pink blankets of skin unwillingly covered her eyes. Just at the edge of the darkness of sleep, a fuzzy image came into focus... *Delbert alone, hitchhiking, skin blistering from the intense desert sun... a huge truck speeding toward him, slowing to a stop with its brakes squealing... Delbert, the flat of his hand protecting his eyes, looking up at the driver who's impatiently waving him aboard... billowing, black smoke attempting to hide the sun as the rumbling truck pulls away.*

Pauline's mind bounded from one scene to the next... *CCC camp... flames leaping out of control... eyes frantically searching for Delbert.*

Straining hard to wake, Pauline frowned at the persistent sight coming into focus... *a slow-moving train approaching... Delbert, face smudged and hat pulled down tight, leaping onto one of the dark black cars, grabbing at the slippery rail.*

Pauline grimaced... *the sound of Delbert's feet landing on the wood floor of the boxcar... wobbly legs apart, balancing... his eyes adjusting to the darkness inside... slowly searching the walls— dark, scarred walls, lined with gaunt-looking men and boys with ashen faces and shadowy eyes... Delbert hanging his head low as if attempting to avoid their stares, now shuffling across the splintery, wood plank floor... wedging himself into a small space between two men smoking... looking relieved, he leans against the wooden slats of the boxcar... sliding down the splintery wall until resting on his haunches—as if ready to flee.*

Try as she might there was no awakening... *black dust clouds swirling around an image of God, His tears forming the long-awaited rain over an endless barren land.*

Pauline stirred, moaning, head swaying from side to side. She strained at heavy lids, struggling as if trying to get all the darkness out. "I don't want to see anymore!" She screamed.

"Pauline? Pauline?" She heard the sweetness of Mama's soft voice calling her. She felt someone persistently shaking her arm. Pauline pried her eyes open to see Mama leaning over the front seat smiling at her in disbelief. "What on earth were you dreaming about, child?"

"Oh Mama, it was a bad dream. Thank you for waking me." Pauline rubbed the deep creases on her cheek where she had been lying on her hand, and attempted to gently shake the numbness from her fingers, "Where are we now, Daddy?"

"Still a good piece from the border sweetheart, yes a good piece. We'll need to stop over a night at Aunt Mary's house for sure."

* * * * *

The sight of Aunt Mary's home was sobering. The eight of them resembled sheep leaping off a step-less porch. The girls waved eagerly, knees bending in time, their smudged faces unaware of the impression they gave. The Sampley children stared at them as if gazing into a mirror.

That evening, after dinner was blessed, Pauline noticed Mama and Daddy taking abnormally small portions of beans and corn bread. She casually glanced at Dale and June to see if they had noticed. They had. Pauline's stomach felt full as if she couldn't eat another bite.

As they drove away the next morning, Pauline sensed an air of uneasiness in the quiet of the car. Mama seemed to realize the family's need for words. She spoke slowly and deliberately. "Aunt Mary and her family were very kind and generous to us, weren't they? She never once, in all her letters, let on how penniless they were. Jack, as soon as we get settled out in California, we must send for them. I know they would have felt bad if we hadn't stopped, but my, oh my, how it hurt us Sampley's to accept one crumb from their table. Yes, they surely practice God's Word, don't they?

"Do not neglect doing good and sharing; for with such sacrifices God is pleased."

Nothing Mama could say could keep Pauline's emotions from flaring. Fighting back tears, she cried out, "They are poor, Mama" —the swelling in Pauline's throat threatened to choke off her words—"I hated it. I hated seein' them that way."

Could this be the way folks see us Sampley's, too?

Pauline prayed a silent prayer. *Father God, bless them for sharin' what little they had. And Father, lead the poor souls into the Land of Milk and Honey the way you have guided us Sampleys. I thank ye... Pauline.*

Back on Route 66, Daddy grimaced and groaned at the sound of a slow hissing escaping from underneath the hood of the car as it coasted to a stop. Without a word, Daddy stepped out of the car and stood at the edge of the road, stretching. His gangly arms reached for heaven and then fluidly fell toward hell.

Pauline expelled a sigh of relief after searching Daddy's eyes for signs of worry and finding only a mischievous glint.

"How wouldja feel 'bout sleeping under the stars tonight, Runt?"

"Oh, Daddy!"

Pauline scrambled across the makeshift car bed and out the back door of the Oakland. She stepped on the back of Daddy's heel as she walked behind him toward the front of the car. He turned to look down at her, rolling his eyes. His aggravation quickly changed to a grin as he slid his arm around her shoulders, saying, "Come on, Runt, let's take a look."

As Daddy lifted the hood, a wave of steam arose, causing him to lurch back, banging his head. "Judas," he shouted.

Pauline fanned at the air with long sweeping motions while hollering, "Judas Priest."

"Pauline, where'd you hear that?"

"Why, from you, Daddy."

"Well, it's best we don't use his name, Runt. He double-crossed Jesus."

"Okay, Daddy."

Standing on tiptoes, she cautiously leaned over the fender of the car. Startled, she felt a yank on the back of her dress collar.

Mama grumbled, "Pauuuline, do you want to get burned?"

Daddy seemed unaware of Mama's intrusion. "I'm a think'n she's got a blown radiator hose," he said while lowering himself to his knees—getting ready to slide under the car.

"Can I go under, too, Daddy?" Asked Pauline.

While Daddy pondered the idea of Pauline assisting him, Mama made the decision for him. "PAULINE... do you hear the hissing sound of steam escaping?

"Yes, Mama."

"We don't need you burned on top of everything else. Go over there and sit with your sister, and let your Daddy do what he has to do!"

Shoulders slumped; Pauline dragged her feet, kicking up small clouds of loose sand.

"And don't drag your feet. You'll wear out your shoes."

"But Mama, they're already worn out."

"Paulineeeee... pleeeease!" Said Mama.

Pauline folded herself onto the running board of the car, staring aimlessly at the ground. She leaned over to snap a branch off of a nearby tumbleweed and began writing her name in the sand. Alarmed at the sound of a car coming, Pauline waved at an approaching jalopy with six children hanging out of the windows. Two of the kids yelled, "California or bust!" She thought, *Well, I guess it's bust for us.*

Pauline remembered what Daddy said, "If they only have one mattress tied on the roof of the car, they must be poor Okies, two mattresses mediocre, and three mattresses—they must be rich."

Pauline noticed the family dog of the poor Okies standing on the running board of the car. The dog's only safeguard was a tattered rope around his neck, tied to the door handle. Pauline could see the muscles in the animal's legs straining to keep its balance on the narrow platform. Nose up and eyes nervously blinking, the dog devotedly awaited assuring eye contact from his master.

As the car disappeared out of sight, Pauline began to take in the raw beauty of her surroundings. The silhouette of sagebrush and cactus against the sunset was just beginning to come to life when the sound of Daddy's voice startled Pauline.

"We've got us a busted hose. I can fix 'er good enough to get us to the next gas station... I think," he said, with a glimmer in his eye and a half-suppressed grin.

"Can I come back over now, Daddy?" Pauline pleaded.

"Yep, come on, Runt."

Pauline watched curiously as Daddy removed his shoe and fumbled in his pocket for his knife. Leaning against the fender of the Oakland, he sliced a strip of leather from the side of his shoe and pulled out the shoestring. Steadily, he wrapped the strip of leather around the leaky radiator hose. Through clenched teeth, and veins bulging in his neck and arms, he secured it tightly. Daddy's voice was raspy, "It's gettin' late folks, we'll make camp here tonight."

The thought of the Sampley's snuggled in their bedrolls around a cozy campfire excited Pauline, "Come on, June, let's go gather some sticks for a campfire."

Firmly setting her book down on her lap, June asked, "Pauline, what's so exciting about sleeping alongside the road—on the ground—with snakes and spiders, and who knows what else?"

"Oh, June, don't be such a pantywaist." She strolled away, hips swaying dramatically.

Mama, eyes pinched together, interrupted, "Pauline, where did you ever hear of such a thing? Pantywaist! Did you hear that, Jack?"

"Yep, I heard, Fay."

"Well, a boy at school said that to me, Mama."

Mama roughly placed her hands on her hips. "So, Pauline, you like hearing yourself talk that way?"

"Well... no, Mama, not really, but June is such a sissy. She never wants to do anything fun at all."

She hollered back half-heartedly, "Sorry, June."

Dale changed the subject. "I'll go with you, Pauline!"

"Oh, alright, Dale."

Pauline was fully aware that Mama and June would be busy unloading the family's tightly packed belongings. *Huh, women's work.* She and Dale strutted off in the direction of the sunset.

"Pauline, do you think rattlesnakes strike at night?"

Pauline's eyeballs became encircled with white, "Ugh, Dale. What would make you bring that up now? For cryin' out loud. Maybe you oughta stay back with the women?"

"Nah, Pauline. I'm not afraid."

"Well, don't be thinkin' up things ta worry 'bout."

Pauline and Dale arrived back at the campsite with small bundles of sticks cradled in their arms.

Mama and June had just finished setting up camp. June stood around with her hands on her hips suggesting a compliment was due. Pauline looked at the familiar bedrolls arranged around the steel tripod that Mama used for cooking over the campfire. She set her twigs down next to the fire pit, knowing full well that Daddy would want to start the fire himself.

After supper, when the sun was just a burnt orange glow on the horizon, the family, except for Daddy, curled up under quilts next to the smoldering embers.

In the darkness, Pauline could barely see Daddy as he leaned against the fender of the Oakland. She rose up on one elbow so she could hear with both ears. Yes, the familiar rustle of the thin, stiff parchment paper, then Daddy reaching inside his pocket for his tobacco pouch. She could envision him carefully licking one edge of a small, rectangular swatch of paper and sprinkling it with a thin line of shredded, tobacco leaves before rolling it tightly. The flicker of a match caught Pauline's eye. Daddy let his head fall way back, and a stream of white smoke formed a halo over the top of his head.

In the morning, Pauline awoke to the sounds of Mama talking to herself while hooking the handle of the coffeepot to the tripod suspended above the campfire. Flames licked at the slender poles. Deep in thought, Mama stirred biscuit dough while humming "I Come to the Garden Alone." She then dropped spoonfuls of the sticky mass onto a warm cast iron skillet. Pauline's hopes of watching the gooey blobs change into light, flaky morsels, later to be flooded in syrup, were snuffed out when Mama slapped an oversized lid on top.

Looking dismayed, Pauline asked, "Mama, tell me I'm not seein' things. We're really having warm biscuits for breakfast this morning?"

"Yes, Pauline, after all, it is Easter Sunday. And by the way, it's not seein'—it's seeing"— Mama kept right on, not seeming to care if anyone was listening or not. "People all over the world are waking up remembering our Lord giving His only Son to die on the cross for our sins—giving us the hope for eternal life. Can't imagine what it would feel like. I know I could never be selfless enough to give up Dale or Delbert for folks I had never even met, not even for one day." Mama took the lid off of the biscuits shaking her head pitifully. "Just can't imagine how anyone could love us that much... no sir."

Pauline wondered too, but since Mama was so sincere, she just nodded, round-eyed. *Sometimes it's hard to be a believer,* she thought, as she headed toward the car.

"I'll get the syrup."

Pauline leaned over the side of Mama's metal laundry tub packed tight with supplies, her limp arms hugging the curved edges of the cool, slightly eroded basin. Eyes closed—she allowed the familiar scent of lye soap to flood her senses. Inhaling deeply, her flared nostrils sought every trace of the biting scent holding all the memories of home.

Startled, she heard June's voice. "Pauline, the biscuits will be cold by the time you get back here with that syrup. What in the world are you doing over there?"

"I'm comin', June." She hurriedly grabbed the tin of syrup. Quickly turning to run back to the family, Pauline tripped, cradling the tin high as if it were a basket of eggs.

"Oh, Pauuuuline," said June, "Now what have you gone and done. How many times has Mama told you to slow down and watch where you're going? Let me see your knees—the poor, bony, things. You've scraped both knees, and worse yet, you have a bloody hole in your dress. You sit here while I get some water to clean you up."

Pauline, pouring syrup on her warm biscuits, cherished her sister's motherly change of attitude. The two of them sat on a rock near the fire while June gently dabbed at Pauline's dirty, raw knees.

Mama and Daddy looked on silently, savoring the rare moment.

Pauline cherished that Easter morning. She drank in the sight of warm biscuits and syrup, the colors of the rising sun hovering over the expansive desert that surrounded them. She closed her eyes and inhaled deeply. *Thank you, God, all is well.*

Daddy's expression was suddenly serious. "Alright, folks. We'd best stay ahead of the heat of the day. Pauline, think you can hobble over there and get me that canvas water bag off the bumper of the car?"

Pauline leaped at the chance to do something that wasn't woman's work. "Can I pour the water into the radiator, too, Daddy?"

"Nope. We can't take a chance of wasting a single drop of this cool, clear water. It's our salvation."

Daddy held the bag with both hands, pouring slowly. He handed the lifeless canvas bag back to Pauline with a look that spoke more than words could say.

"There, now that should get us a ways. I just hope my patch job holds 'til we can get us a new hose and some more water up the road apiece. Reminds me of that Bob Nolan song, "Cool, Clear Water."

> *All day I've faced a barren waste*
> *Without the taste of water, cool water.*
> *Old Dan and I with throats burnt dry*
> *And souls that cry for water,*
> *Cool, clear water.*

The whole family joined in, singing and swaying to the tune.

Chapter Ten

At the gas station, the attendant's eyes darted from one fender to the other as he guided Daddy, driving the Oakland between the two posts supporting the garage. His hand moved at a snail's pace as if it were hinged to his wrist. Suddenly, he pressed the flat of his palm toward them, fingers tense and stretched apart. "Whoah."

Nearly hypnotized, Pauline and June studied the fellow who looked to be about 18 with dark, slicked-back hair, electric-blue eyes, rolled up sleeves revealing eye-catching muscle definition. Caught off guard, the girls turned away blushing, as he smiled at them before speaking to Daddy.

"You can all hop out now while I check things out. From the way your radiator is a steamin' I suspect you're probably right thinkin' it's a hose. There's a Coke machine 'round the corner. Shouldn't take too long to get 'er back on the road."

The Sampley's filed out of the car, straining and stretching. Curious, Pauline watched as the raven-haired fellow eyed June. June's only response to his obvious interest was an ever so slight smile, while intently brushing something off of her shoe. The outgoing young man was getting plenty of unwanted attention from Daddy though. Pauline had never before seen such a stone-faced glare on his face.

Pauline walked around the corner and spotted the Coke machine. She read the painted sign on the cooler: *The pause that refreshes— Coca-Cola.* She closed her eyes and leaned back, molding her spine to the curve of the cool, red metal. Pauline remembered tasting a Coke once. She could easily imagine how her parched throat would benefit from the thirst-quenching sweetness. June joined her, resting the flat of one foot against the side and running her fingers through her shoulder length brunette hair.

Having momentarily forgotten the grease-smudged attendant, Pauline and June were both startled when they realized he was once again close-by. Their eyes trailed the tan, muscular arm that seemed to be pushing hard against the Coke machine that June's backside rested against. He looked directly into June's eyes. "Buy you a Coke?"

Just as Pauline was about to speak, June gave her a hidden pinch. Pauline whispered loudly, "Ouch!"

Just then Daddy stepped around the corner. "Girls, the both of you git the water bag from the front bumper of the car and fill it. We need to be on our way jest as soon as this here young fella fixes our car." Daddy glared at the red-faced boy who quickly headed toward the hood of the Oakland.

Pauline and June obediently hooked the rope handle of the bag over a water outlet that stood on the shady side of the garage. When the sides of the canvas bulged slightly and the water ran over the top, they screwed the metal lid on tight and hung it back in its place.

Pauline thought to herself, although she would never want

Daddy to know, she was dying for one of those Cokes. If there was one thing she couldn't stand though, it was seeing the hurt in Daddy's eyes when he couldn't give them something they wanted. To her surprise she heard Daddy holler, "Fay, don't we have a little change for the Sampley family to share one of them there Coca-Colas?"

Mama grumbled and refused to taste the sweet treat, complaining, "I can't believe you would put something in your body, God's temple, that was intended to be a nerve and tonic stimulant!"

* * * * *

As far as Pauline could see, Route 66 now stretched through an open plain of nothingness. The afternoon heat had set in, and within the boundaries of the Oakland, the air was stifling. Pauline felt as if her legs were on pins and needles, and her skin was crawling. The last thing she was interested in was Mama's handy assortment of schoolwork, singing, or storytelling. Glancing out the window again, Pauline spotted a signpost up ahead.

"Look Mama... why would there be a road sign way out here in the middle of nowhere?"

"Well, I can't imagine, sweetheart?"

Everyone seemed to perk-up with curiosity as they drove closer to the oddity. Squinting, Mama read:

WITHIN THIS VALE...

Puzzled, June mumbled, "Within this vale?"

Daddy scratched his head. "Within this vale? Why, if that ain't the most peculiar thing I ever saw?"

Pauline's eyes bulged. "Kinda mysterious, huh?"

Deep in thought, the family sat in silence until Pauline shouted, "Well, I'll be doggone if there ain't another one just up the road a piece."

Mama's voice was harsh, "Pauline, how many times do I have to tell you, 'ain't' is not a word."

An air of excitement filled the car, and Pauline could tell that Daddy's foot was heavy on the accelerator.

June read the next postings:

OF TOIL AND SIN...

YOUR HEAD GROWS BALD...

BUT NOT YOUR CHIN... Burma Shave

Daddy removed his hat and ran his hand across the top of his head. "Well, I'll be, if that ain't something. Whoops, guess Pauline talks like me, don't she kids?" He shot a guilty glance toward Mama.

Not long after the giggling subsided, Pauline leaned forward resting her arms on the back of Mama's shoulders. "Within this vale, of toil and sin, your head grows bald, but not your chin, Burma Shave." Mouth askew, Pauline asked, "What's Burma Shave, Mama?"

Dale raised his hand as if he was sitting in a schoolroom. "I know what Burma Shave is— Delbert told me. He said he always wished he could try some. It's a shaving cream that rich people use, instead of swishing a brush around in a cup of soap like Daddy does."

Mama smiled as if she were trying to stifle a hearty laugh. "Good for you, Dale. Good English, too."

Pauline moved her lips mimicking Mama's compliment to Dale, then settled on a spiteful grin.

June leaned forward with her chin resting on Daddy's shoulder. "Look, there's another one! Can I read this one?"

Pauline was glad June volunteered to read. *I would never volunteer to read — I hate hearing myself stammer and stutter.*

Mama seemed relieved that something was diverting the attention from their growing boredom. "Alright, June, get ready... here it comes."

THE BEARDED LADY...

TRIED A JAR...

SHE'S NOW...

A FAMOUS...

MOVIE STAR... Burma Shave

Every one now sat upright in their seats anticipating the next jingle. Shoulders were no longer drooping from boredom. Eyes were pinned on the desolate road ahead.

THE ANSWER TO...

A MAIDEN'S...

PRAYER...

IS NOT A CHIN...

OF STUBBY...

HAIR...Burma Shave

After the laughter subsided, Mama turned to Pauline.

"Pauline, it'll be your turn to read next. Okay?"

Pauline rolled her eyes and cringed. *I know what Mamas up to.* She began searching the opposite side of the road. *Maybe she'll think I didn't see them, or maybe there won't be any more?*

"Pauline, watch now, I think I see something up ahead."

"Oh really, Mama, I don't see a thing..."

"Pauline you can do this. Now be ready."

"Your sh... sh...sh...sh"

"Shaving, Pauline."

YOUR SHAVING BRUSH...

HAS HAD IT'S DAY...

SO WHY NOT...

SHAVE THE moMO.. MO.. MO.. WAY"

"'Modern,' Pauline."

"Okay, I got it, Mama. Your shaving brush has had its day, so why not shave the modern way, Burma Shave."

Everyone cheered and clapped while Pauline cocked her chin, raising both fists high.

Dale excitedly shouted, "Daddy, your turn to read the next one."

Pauline cut him off with a jab to the rib. She quickly cupped her hand around Dale's ear, looking at him through tightly squinted eyes. She whispered angrily into his ear, "Dale, you know. Daddy can't read!"

June eagerly announced, "There's another one!"

BENEATH THIS STONE...

LIES ELMER GUSH...

TICKLED TO DEATH...

BY HIS...

SHAVING BRUSH... Burma Shave

Daddy quickly lifted his right hand from the back of Mama's seat and held the steering wheel with both hands. "I'm gonna pull 'er over up ahead. I heard tell there might be water barrels along the way. Think I just spotted one up yonder. Looks like some other folks is doin' the same. We can't take a chance on our radiator a runnin' dry again."

The brakes squealed as Daddy stopped the Oakland next to a rusty barrel with the word water barely visible on one side.

Pauline asked, "Mama, why would that other car be heading away from the California border?" Mama hushed her.

Daddy held the rim of his hat between his thumb and forefinger and nodded at the scraggly man hobbling toward the barrel. Daddy stretched his arm forward to shake the hand of the stranger. "Jack Sampley," he said as the two clasped hands tightly.

The stranger's voice was hoarse. "Harry Wilson. You must be headed to California, eh?"

Daddy stared into the man's eyes; searching for the answer he feared getting. "Yep, seems most folks is headed toward the 'Promised Land' these days."

Caught up in the situation, Pauline gazed at the glum, hollow-eyed family, aware of their stringy hair and soiled clothes. Four young stair step girls walked over to lean against the barrel, seemingly unconcerned about the rust rubbing off onto their dresses.

As they visited, Daddy ladled water into the stranger's bag first, letting the overflow splash back into the barrel.

"Yeah, we made it to the Land of Milk and Honey, but it sure weren't what we s'pected. No siree. Still got the handbill in the car telling us 'bout all the work out there in sunny California. 'One-thousand Pea Pickers Needed.' Still can't believe it. Ended up in a squatter's camp next to a canal. People was a sufferin' from rickets. Imagine that in a land where fruit was s'pose to be growin' everywhere a body turned? Tuberculosis, diphtheria, and measles were killin' folks off, too. Wife and I buried two sons in that camp. Couldn't even give 'em a decent burial. My wife has barely spoken a word since.

"Them California farmers is smart! They know that the more pickers that show, the less pay they'll put out. Too many came, that's all, jest too many. It's a joke. An' those Californians, they'd jest as soon spit on ya as give one of us 'Okies' a good paying job."

* * * * *

Not a word was spoken as the two families parted company.

It was when the sun was about to touch the horizon that Daddy finally spoke, "Think we'll pull off the road up ahead and make camp for the night." Deep in thought, Daddy slowly turned his head from side to side, finally speaking, "Those poor, pitiful souls we met back there at the watering hole sure makes us realize how blessed we are to have Uncle Charlie and Aunt Julia waitin' on us. Right kids? Yes, that sure makes all the difference, don't it? Now, tomorrow, I want all three of you to watch for that border crossing. Tomorrow's the day. Lord willin' and the creek don't rise."

* * * * *

Pauline pulled her quilt over the top of her head in an attempt to block the brightness of dawn. Looking up toward the sun through her worn quilt, reminded her of a kaleidoscope someone showed her once when she was very young—the colors danced and glimmered. When her eyes began to cross from the closeness of the quilt, she peeled it from her face, releasing the heat of her breath.

Blinking in an attempt to focus, Pauline caught sight of Mama and Daddy starting the cook fire for breakfast. The heat rose in a blur of waves, inviting her mind to reel back to the past... the soddy... harvesting cotton and beets... Delbert screaming... blood running down his hand... the letter to Aunt Julia. She visualized the reply... *The mine here in the Mojave Desert has given your Uncle a steady job with fair pay. You all are welcome to keep house with us until you get back on your feet.*

Pauline felt a sickening feeling of fear flowing through her. The family they met at the water barrel last night. *What if California closes the border and won't let anyone else cross? It was nearly a year ago when I received that letter from Aunt Julia, and now we're seeing cars driving away from the border crossing!*

Closing her eyes, she shook her head, ridding herself of those haunting thoughts and absorbed in blissful anticipation of a new life, and how different it would be.

Pauline felt as if her smile had a mind of its own. Her lips spread widely over the protrusion of her teeth and seemed to stick there. She looked at the faces of the rest, eyes alive and eager, searching for any sign of the border station. They ignored the tired looking cars passing them going the other direction, refusing to allow their spirits to be crushed.

Mama spoke nervously, "What's that up ahead, Jack?"

As they pulled closer, they saw a line of dusty cars leading to a building with a lean-to on one side. About one in every three cars was making a U-turn.

Pauline rested her chin on the window frame of the Oakland, staring at the faces of the exiting families as they drove past. *That's bare-boned, lick-the-dust-pitiful,* she thought!

The Oakland rolled to a stop near a sign reading "Barstow City Limits." Pauline grew tense as she eyed the furrowed brows and wide eyes on the faces of the others.

Two officials approached the driver's side of the car. Daddy tipped his hat and smiled. Lips strained, he greeted them. "Howdy."

The dark-skinned guard did not reply but instead peered into the car, his brown eyes searching. "Got any fruit or vegetables on board. We don't want anyone bringing disease into the Sunshine State," he said with a smirk.

They asked everyone to step out and stand aside while they sifted through the contents with quick, jerky movements and stern faces, disturbing what had been the Sampley's home on wheels.

June began to whimper, "What are we going to do?"

Pauline scooted close in an attempt to comfort her. "June, you know we don't have any fruit or vegetables, don't you? After all, we haven't had any for weeks."

"Yesssss, butttt "

Mama interrupted eyeing the guards, "Yes, that's right, we haven't a thing to worry about."

Pauline felt as if short red hackles were standing up on the back of her neck.

One guard backed himself out of the car. "Okay, you can get

back in." Sensing their hurried pace, everyone quickly climbed into their places. The children settled themselves on top of their now cluttered belongings.

The guard spoke gruffly, "Pull up!"

Daddy pulled the Oakland forward. He reached into his back pocket, pulling out a paper-thin wallet with rough, worn edges. Through half-opened lids, the family watched Daddy count out nearly all that was left of their Oshkosh savings. The guard sighed as Daddy slapped the last dollar into his hand.

The only sound breaking the silence as they drove off was the grumbling voices of the officers, "Okie trash!"

Daddy kept both hands steady on the steering wheel until the border station was clearly out of sight. Then, slowing to a stop off the side of the road, he wiped the sweat from his forehead and pretended to fling it out the window. The family erupted with laughter.

Everyone cried out in unison, "We made it!"

Chapter Eleven

It was the winter of 1938. Pauline felt the sun burning her scalp through the erratic parts in her hair. She sat upright, legs crossed on her bedroll, cringing as she cupped both hands over her head — knowing full well that her scalp would soon be covered with a crossroad of blisters. One hand lifted an edge of her quilt, creating a teepee of shade. She stared out at the barren desert shouting out to anyone who would listen, "So if this is California, why does it look just like the other side of the border?"

Seeming oblivious to Pauline's question, Mama squinted, shielding her face from the harsh sunlight with the flat of her hand. "No breakfast this morning kids, at least not until we stop for gas up ahead — should be a General Store there."

Pauline jumped up enthusiastically. "Oh well, this is the last time we'll pack the car again for a while. Bet I can beat ya rolling up the bedrolls, June."

"Who cares, you little ruunnttt! I can't believe how little it takes to keep you entertained!"

Mama glared at June with a frown. "June, I need to see you up and pitching in—right now!"

* * * * *

As the car vibrated over the washboard road, Pauline tried to hide the wooziness of her stomach—but Mama noticed. "Pauline, you're as pale as a ghost. Are you about to get sick? Do you want Daddy to pull over?"

"No, I'll be fine," Pauline pressed her hand tight to her stomach and filled her cheeks with air. She released the air slowly and deliberately, eyes closed.

Mama looked worried. "Open your eyes and focus on something."

"Mama, there aint' nothin' to focus on. Oooooh, sorry for saying aint' again, must be my weak state of misery.

"Just focus on the horizon, Pauline. Do you want Daddy to pull over?"

Pauline found the look of apprehension on June's face annoying. She opened her eyes periodically to see June's electric blue eyes glaring at her, as if her sickness were contagious, while slowly sliding as far away as she could get, pulling Dale with her.

"Pauline, whatever you do, don't get sick on us, okay?"

"Thanks. Ya really care about me don't ya, June?"

"Well, you know what a mess it would make if you got sick in the car... don't you, Pauline?"

"Daddy, you'd best pull over."

"Okay, now ya jest hold on, honey. I'll pull the car over right away."

The car screeched to a stop. Through closed eyes, Pauline flinched as Daddy's open arms proceeded to lift her out of the car. "Oh Daddy, ya don't have to carry me, I can walk." Out of the corner of her eye, she saw Mama running around the front of the car handing June a cloth.

Anxiously, Mama called to June, "Use the water from the radiator bag to dampen this cloth for her forehead, and don't spill any!"

Pauline caught a look of concern on June's face.

After each bout of vomit and then dry heaves, Pauline felt Daddy firmly press the warm cloth against her forehead. She cupped her head in her hands. Sitting next to her on the running board of the car, Daddy wrapped one arm around Pauline's shoulders.

Daddy hollered for June, who stood with her back turned to the whole event, "June, rinse this cloth and wet it again."

June held two fingers out and reached for a corner of the cloth with her pinchers—nose scrunched, she took deep breaths while looking away.

Daddy's eyelids drooped, halfway hiding his gray eyes. "Honey, ya hang on now. Yer jest car sick—jest too much ridin' on an empty stomach. I'm jest sure there'll be a store up ahead. Then we'll get ya somethin' in that stomach of yours."

"Okay, Daddy, I think I can make it now."

* * * * *

While Daddy filled the car with gas, Pauline, June, and Mama used the rearview mirror to comb their hair. Pauline noticed her face was chalk white and her hands were trembling. Mama patted Pauline's wrist. "You sure you don't want to just wait in the car, honey?"

"No, Mama. I'll be alright. Besides, I think I need to stand up and walk a bit."

Stepping out of the Oakland, the three attempted to smooth the wrinkles out of their dresses before looking for a grocery store.

June's shoulders straightened, and her eyes brightened. "Mama, looks like there's a little store right across the street — next to that feed store."

Mama opened the creaky screen door, and the threesome stepped inside. They eyed the dark walls stacked with canned goods, flour, sugar and other staples. A plump woman stood in the doorway of the attached living room, ironing. "Can I help you?"

Mama, finger pressed against her chin, eyed a round of bologna in the cooler. Shoulders back and head high, she asked, "How much would five thin slices of baloney and five slices of bread cost?"

The lady looked at Mama over the rim of her glasses.

"Five slices of bread?"

Pauline shifted her weight as she felt the woman's eyes studying her inch by inch before turning her attention back to Mama. "Bread comes in a loaf you know."

"Yes I know, but I would like to buy five pieces."

"Um, I guess I could take five slices from an open loaf in my kitchen."

"I'd be obliged. How much will that be?"

"That'll be five cents."

"And the baloney?"

"Um, twenty-five cents, I guess."

Mama mumbled as she opened her familiar coin purse, "Now

let's see, five plus twenty-five equals thirty." Her proud blue-gray eyes seemed to connect with the woman as if Mama could see right through her. "Here's thirty cents, thank you, you're so very kind. Let's go girls."

Mama pivoted around with a noticeable clicking of her heels on the worn, wooden floor and walked toward the screen door, holding it open for June and Pauline. With her pocketbook and package in one hand, she gently wrapped her free arm around Pauline's waist as she escorted both girls across the squeaky, plank board porch.

Mama, Pauline, and June walked back to the service station where Daddy and Dale stood in the garage visiting with the owner.

With the car doors wide open, Pauline and Dale sat on the running board of the car, looking longingly at Mama's package that was neatly wrapped and tied with red string. Pauline pulled her dress down over her knees, as Mama's look dictated.

Mama stood in front of June, and with a familiar nod, motioned to June to place her hands together, palms up. She laid a piece of bread and baloney on her ready-made table and folded it over—one for each family member. "This will have to tide us over until we get to Uncle Charlie's and Aunt Julia's."

That means we're out of money, thought Pauline.

The inviting morsel was about to touch Pauline's lips when Mama began to pray, "Father God, we praise you for this food and ask that it nourish our bodies. We pray that you guide every step we take. In the precious name of Jesus, Amen."

The meal was quiet until June moaned, "I sure hope Uncle Charlie and Aunt Julia live in the city."

Pauline replied sharply. "What's there to do in the city anyway?

Houses and cars, cars and houses, and people. People we don't know."

"There's plenty to do in the city, Pauuuuliinnne!"

"Ah, how would you know? Yav've never even lived in a city!"

"I read about such things. That's how I know!"

Mama, sitting between the two girls, scowled. "Girls, will you please try to get along?"

Looking down at the sand, Pauline whispered, "Alright, Mama. I'm sorry." She intently turned to June, checking for any obvious form of remorse. Frustrated, she stomped one foot and walked away.

* * * * *

Rubbing her neck from sleeping propped up against the backseat window, Pauline groggily asked, "Mama, what's that?" Her eyes focused on a ramshackle shanty, silhouetted by the sliver of a moon.

"Well, honey, that must be Uncle Charlie and Aunt Julia's place."

The car slowed as everyone stared at the warped clapboard-sided house and the leaning porch propped up by a two-by-four braced against one corner.

June cried, "Mama, it's just an old shack out here in the middle of the desert."

Daddy spoke sternly, "Truth is, June, it ain't what we was expectin', but I'll guarantee ya things will look a whole lot better in the light of day. We sure as heck ain't got no right to ask fer more than ya Aunt and Uncle a sharin' what they got with us, leastways 'til we can stand on our own two feet again. Now hear me, and hear me good. I won't have any of my youngin's a crossin' the threshold of these kind folks' home without a thankful heart. And there ain't a one of ya too old to take out behind the shed if need be. Course, I would never s'pect that of a Sampley..."

Pauline thought that Aunt Julia and Uncle Charlie looked like she remembered... just older.

An aroma of beans and corn bread filled Aunt Julia's kitchen. Crowding around the table and listening to the adults retell stories of the past, made Pauline feel safe and seemed to fill something deep inside that she didn't know was empty. *It's good,* she thought.

After dinner, Aunt Julia showed the Sampley's to the feed house that would become their sleeping quarters. The chicken coop didn't look much different than the main house. Clearly, it had never seen a paintbrush and the dry, warped, wood siding allowed fragments of moonlight to filter through.

Pauline awoke early the next morning to the clucking, scratching, and pecking of chickens and geese. She studied the sleeping faces of the others. The sun was peaking through the warped, sideboard walls and bouncing off the white streaks in Mama's hair. *How does she manage to look so sweet, even when she is sleeping?* Daddy still looked like he did when he was in the hospital with dust pneumonia—complexion sallow, cheeks sunken. June resembled a ruffled barn owl—her dark, stick-straight hair standing on end. I wish I had June's clear, china doll complexion, not a freckle to her name. And Dale, young and innocent, lips slightly parted, emitted a barely audible snore.

Pauline tiptoed across the damp dirt floor. She stifled her moans as she hobbled across previously spilled grain that pricked her bare feet. Slowly, she opened the feed house door just a crack. In a flash, chickens and geese rushed toward her clucking and squawking, pushing their way past her toward the grain sacks stacked in the corner.

Everyone seemed to grumble at the same time. "What's going on? Who let them in?"

"Pauline what did you do? Get them out! Get them out!"

Pauline immediately jumped back into her bedroll, covered her head and screamed, "Daddy! Help! Help!"

"What on earth is going on? Did you open the door, Pauline?"

"Yes, Daddy, get them out. Get them out of here, pleeease!"

Even though her quilt, Pauline felt the sharp claws of the chickens. She heard the unnerving flapping of wings. Then, peering out from under one corner, she saw Daddy herding the hungry mob out the door by waving his blanket from side to side.

"Oh, thank you, Daddy. I just wanted to see what was outside. I didn't know they were all waiting."

It took a moment of silence for everyone to digest what just happened. Daddy's face was flushed, and he looked younger than Pauline had seen him look in a long time. Pauline wondered, *Is Daddy angry with me?* Suddenly, he threw his head back and succumbed to a roar of laughter, followed by giggles and happy tears from the rest of the family.

When everyone was reduced to breathlessness, Mama looked around wide-eyed. "If this is to be our new sleeping quarters, it will need a good cleaning."

Everyone seemed to immediately freeze at the thought of Mama's seriousness until another wave of laughter washed over them.

Daddy and the children watched Mama with curiosity as she strutted over the tops of tousled blankets and quilts to give a determined tug on a heavy string that secured one of the feedbags. "Here, I'll throw those fine feathered friends some grain so we can open the door and see exactly where we are in the daylight. Here chick, chick, chick."

After the poultry were safely hunting and pecking, everyone clustered around the door, staring out silently. June rolled her eyes. "Tumbleweed and sand—and tumbleweed."

*****

Over a breakfast of biscuits and gravy, Pauline listened intently to Uncle Charlie, his eyelids moist and swollen. "Lord knows Jack, I hate to tell ya this, but when Julia wrote back to Pauline, Jesus be my witness, I was sure there was work for ya here. Then jest two days ago, they tell us that the Borax Mine over in Boron is a-layin' off workers. Came as a shock to everyone. So, as not to leave us totally out in the cold, they told us we might find work farther out west, a-pickin' oranges 'round Bakersfield."

Pauline felt her eyes widen and realized she was holding her breath. Through the uncomfortable silence, she watched Uncle Charlie roll his head from side-to-side as his shoulders drooped lower and lower. Then she felt her attitude shift to one of hope as Uncle Charlie looked directly into Daddy's eyes and spoke firmly, "I thought we could head out first thing in the morning if that's okay with you?" Uncle Charlie's small, lean form stood as he pushed his chair back. "Y'all are welcome to stay here as long as need be. What's ours is yours."

"Charlie, I'm not even gonna try ta tell ya we ain't disappointed, but we sure as heck got no cause to blame ya or nobody else. Ya did yer best and that's all a guy can ask. Guess it's jest gonna take a while before our ol' buddy Roosevelt gets things turned around. You bet I'll head out with ya in the mornin'. At this point pickin' oranges sounds mighty appealin'! We jest need a little time to get our feet on the ground again... jest a little time."

For what seemed like ages, the only sound was the rocking back and forth of the crate that Pauline was sitting on. She was almost unaware of the crude sort of rhythm. She studied a ribbon of light streaking through the cloudy, cracked, kitchen window, highlighting Aunt Julia's familiar gravy bowl with worn gold trim and faded yellow roses. From underneath the table, she felt the firm pat of Mama's hand on her knee, sending her a strong message to sit still.

Unable to withstand her boredom a minute longer, Pauline spoke up, "Aunt Julia, I saw an old truck travelin' fast across the desert this morning. I was wonderin'...."

"Sweetheart, that was probably your Cousin Lindell. When we first moved here that rusty ol' pickup truck had been left out behind the chicken coop. During better times, Lindell had himself a job in town. Bought some parts to get that ol' eyesore runnin'".

"We insist he stay in school though, as long as we can scrape enough gas money together for him to get there and back. Look at him now, racing across the desert as if he don't have a brain in his head. Guess we spoiled him when times was good. He needs to learn a thing or two about waste not want not. He drives that truck all over tarnation, but that will come to a standstill now!"

Pauline swiveled around on her crate just in time to see Lindell's truck consumed by a flurry of sand as he completed a figure eight.

"Can I go out and see Lindell, Mama? Can I?"

While Mama was contemplating her answer, Pauline excitingly

ran out the front door.

Stumbling over a loose board on the sloping front porch, Pauline jumped off the edge, waving her arms in the air and shouting, "Cousin Lindell! Cousin Lindell!" Her heart raced as she watched him drive up and down the sandy mounds, then turn toward her, leaving a trail of dust behind him.

Pauline ran across the sand as if in slow motion, arms weak from the constant waving. At last, the truck slowed and pulled up next to her. She quickly leaned across the rolled down the window of the car. Out of breath and throat hoarse from yelling, she gasped. "Lindell, it's me, yer Cousin Pauline."

"Well, I'll be. Ya finally got here, Runt! Hop in. I'll take ya fer a spin."

As Pauline slid across the dusty seat, she thought she must be dreaming. Just me and Cousin Lindell, racing off across the desert...

Pauline admired Lindell as he wrapped the palm of his hand around the well-worn shift knob that protruded out of the floor between the two of them. Shifting into gear, he pressed the accelerator pedal to the floor while letting up on the clutch. Tires spinning and spitting on the loose sand, they were off, dodging sagebrush, aiming at the horizon, hair twirling and blowing. Pauline propped her neck on the seat back allowing the aroma of the early morning dew on the parched land to fill her nostrils.

Safely away from the house, Lindell skidded to a stop. The stillness provided a sharp contrast to the throbbing of the engine. The thumping of Pauline's heart began to calm as the two of them sat in silence. Lindell spoke without turning to look at her, attempting to conceal a slight grin. "Wanna take the wheel, Pauline?"

Instantly, the pounding of her heart resumed, causing her voice to quiver nervously.

"Ssurre, I want to take the w-wheeel."

Lindell reached through the open window, lifting one leg at a time over the rope that secured the broken door handle to something hidden under the seat.

Pauline slid across to the driver's seat and grasped the steering wheel with both hands. "Ummm, there's only one thing, Lindell, I've never driven a car before, 'cept while sitting on Daddy's lap when I was little... but I've watched aplenty!"

Lindell shook his head and sighed regretfully. "Okay, push the clutch all the way down."

The look on Lindell's face made Pauline nervous. *I hope he is not going to take his offer back.*

"The—the clutch?"

Lindell rolled his eyes while stretching his foot around the stick shift and gently tapping the clutch pedal, avoiding eye contact with Pauline.

"Oh, okay."

Pauline scooted forward in the seat until her toes reached the pedal. Lindell groaned, rolling his jacket up and stuffing it behind Pauline's lower back.

"I'm starting to wish I'd never started this," he complained half-heartedly. "Now, when ya can move the stick right and left freely, like this, yer in neutral." Pauline shook her head obediently. "Push the shift straight up into first, and then slowly let the clutch out while giving it the gas."

Pauline was pushing the clutch in so tightly with her toes that her leg was beginning to tremble. She began releasing the pressure, easing the tension on her calf muscle. She clenched her teeth, flashing her eyes over at Lindell as the engine sputtered and died.

"Try again."

Pauline sighed as once more the engine sputtered and died.

"Try again," Lindell said while staring off in the distance.

Suddenly the truck lunged forward, causing Pauline to tighten her grip on the steering wheel. After a couple of hard jerks they began weaving off across the desert.

Lindell lunged his fist high into the air. "Yahoo!"

* * * * *

Monday morning, Daddy and Uncle Charlie left for Bakersfield. Mama and Aunt Julia waved the children off to school with Lindell in charge of getting everyone to class. June rode in the front seat, and Pauline and Dale obediently sat in the truck-bed.

The familiar butterflies returned to the pit of Pauline's stomach. The teacher seemed a blur. The single thing that caught Pauline's attention throughout the whole day was mention of a "Can Dance." Her curiosity was peaked, but not to the point of raising her hand to ask, *What is a Can Dance?*

I'll ask Lindell on the way home, she thought.

Lindell leaned against the door, waiting for his passengers to appear one by one. Pauline was the first to arrive, but she could tell he preferred that she wasn't seen standing too close. She boosted herself up to where there had, at one time, been a tailgate. Without turning to look at him, Pauline asked, "Lindell, do ya know what a Can Dance is?"

"Oh Pauline, ya don't know nothin', do ya? The school's havin' one Saturday night. Why don't ya come and find out? I'll tell ya one thing though, ya'll have to bring a can of food fer the poor people in order to get in!"

"Ya mean we're not the poor people?" Pauline asked with a puzzled cock of her head.

1930s DUSTBOWL IMAGES

The Migrant Mother *by Dorothea Lange*

The Dust Bowl forced tens of thousands of poverty-stricken families to abandon their farms, unable to pay mortgages or grow crops. Many of these families, who were often known as "Okies" because so many of them came from Oklahoma, migrated to California and other states to find that the Great Depression had rendered economic conditions there little better than those they had left behind.

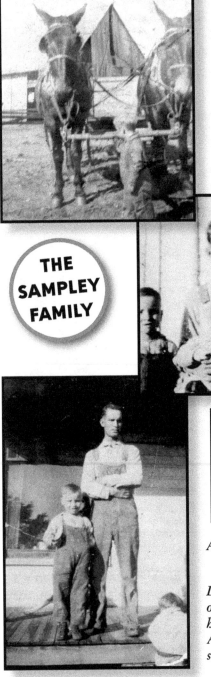

Left: Nellie and Ol' Dan, the two mules the Sampley family had on their Texas homestead, circa early 1930 – probably Dale holding the harness.

Below L-R: Back - Daddy, Mama; Front - Delbert, Dale (in Daddy's lap), June and Pauline, circa 1926, before the onset of the Dustbowl era. Probably taken in Washita, Co, OK prior to moving to Texas.

THE SAMPLEY FAMILY

Above: An Oakland car.

Left: Delbert and Daddy, circa 1930, on the porch of the Sears Roebuck house owned by Uncle Charlie and Aunt Julia. Probably Pauline on the step, lower right.

Florence "Pancho" Barnes poses with her Travelair Model R Mystery Ship, most likely at Van Nuys Airport. In August 1930, she broke Amelia Earhart's Women's air speed record in this aircraft.

In 1935, Barnes originally purchased the property where the club would later stand to grow alfalfa, raise pigs and cattle and start a dairy. As the nearby U.S. Army Air Corps base at Muroc Army Air Base expanded in the post World War II period, the ranch's other business as a restaurant, bar, and hotel quickly outgrew its humble beginnings.

Barnes' life was chronicled in a 2009 documentary film for PBS station KOCE-TV, entitled The Legend of Pancho Barnes and the Happy Bottom Riding Club.

A made-for-TV movie aired on the CBS TV network, Pancho Barnes *(1988), starring Valerie Bertinelli, featured a fictionalized version of Barnes' life and events relating to The Happy Bottom Riding Club.*

On their trek west, the Sampley Family worked at the Pancho Barnes Ranch.

1930s DUSTBOWL IMAGES

THE SAMPLEY FAMILY

Above: Pauline and June, Pancho Barnes Ranch, near Edwards Air Force Base in the Mojave Desert, circa 1937. Just below June's elbow, on the right, someone is photobombing the shot!!!

Left: Daddy, Harley "Jack" Sampley. Pancho Barnes Ranch.

Right: Woman in an ad shows off a wringer washer, much like the one Mama had in Long Beach, CA.

1930s DUSTBOWL IMAGES

Above: A dust storm engulfs a town.

Right: Child working in a cotton field during the Dustbowl.

Below: Had to wash your feet every night before bed.

Above L-R: Back - Daddy, Delbert, Dale; Front - June, Pauline, Mama (Neva Fay) in Long Beach, CA, in the early 1940s.

Below: A reunion at Uncle Charlie's and Aunt Julia's in the Mojave Desert in the late 1930s. L-R: Dale, Uncle Charlie, Charles, Delbert, and Daddy.

THE SAMPLEY FAMILY

1930s DUSTBOWL IMAGES

Above: Newspaper insulation on the walls.

Above: Tent in a migrant camp.

Right: The migration to California.

Below: Charles Jones Jr., US Navy Seabees, with his daughter.

Above: June Sampley and Charles Jones Jr., married in Las Vegas, NV, on July 21, 1939.

Below: Fay Sampley in her backyard garden on Lemon St., Long Beach, CA, in early 1940.

Right: Lavaliere.

THE SAMPLEY FAMILY

Left: Dust bowl refugees on the highway near Bakersfield, California, 1935. Photo by Dorothea Lange.

Below: Woman in a slat bonnet hoes a drought-stricken garden.

1930s DUSTBOWL IMAGES

Left: Desolate farm near Dalhart, TX in 1938—much like Uncle Charlie Sampley's place.

Right: A dust storm engulfs the main street of a small town during the 1930s.

1930s DUSTBOWL IMAGES

Left: A migrant tent camp similar to many others across California in the 1930s.

Above: A sod-roofed house known as a "soddy."

Left: A child labors in a cotton field during the 1930s.

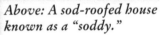

Right: a lone car races ahead of a dust storm over the flat landscape during the 1930s dust bowl.

1930s DUSTBOWL IMAGES

Californians tried to stop migrants from moving into their state by creating checkpoints on main highways called "Bum Blockades". They even instated an anti-Okie law which punished anyone bringing in "indigents" with jail time. A Los Angeles Times *article dated March 9, 2003 read: "The City of Angels had built itself by luring migrants west to sunny skies and balmy temperatures. But its attitude took a 180-degree turn during the Great Depression as jobs dried up and thousands of unemployed overwhelmed the city. Many civic leaders viewed police as a way to stem a transient tide estimated as high as 100,000 a year. Many were deterred by the three dollar charge at the border for a California drivers license."*

Sampley Family Tree

Harley Louis "Jack" Sampley
1894-1954
Born in Oklahoma
Age at death: 60 years
Long Beach, California

Married for life

Neva Fay Sampley
1901 - 1956
Born in Nebraska
Age at death: 55 years
Long Beach, California

Delbert Sampley
1919-1978
Age at death: 59 years
Born in Oklahoma
Married to Hilda
Long Beach, California
United States Army Veteran

June Sampley
1921-1966
Age at death: 45 years
Born in Oklahoma
Married for life to
Charles R. Jones Jr.
United States Navy Veteran

Oleta Pauline Sampley
1923-2001
Age at death: 78 years
Born in Oklahoma
Married for life to
Doyal Blair
Long Beach, California

Dale L. Sampley
1925-1985
Age at death: 60 years
Born in Oklahoma
Married for life to
Geraldine B. Warren
Long Beach, California
United States Army Veteran

Chapter Twelve

Delbert is lucky—he doesn't have to go to school. Wish I could join the CCC. No girls allowed, though. Working in the beet fields instead of going to school has set us so far behind—we'll never catch up. Even bookworm June is burning the midnight oil.

Homework to Pauline spelled drudgery—wasted time that was better spent on answering the call of the wild.

Pauline's eyes easily strayed from her book to a yellowed picture hanging cockeyed next to the kitchen table. *Why did no one ever bother to straighten it?* She studied the scene: a Collie, on a hilltop, fur glistening in the moonlight. The sorrowful look of the dog's eyes, standing over an injured lamb lying in the snow, made her sad. *It's like us Sampleys—needin' someone to rescue us.* She imagined the Collie howling toward the sheepherder and wondered if the lamb was saved or if it eventually died. The picture made her think of Psalm 23.

* * * * *

Pauline found it difficult to talk to Mama about the Can Dance. She hadn't spoken of such things before and could just envision Mama gasping and holding her hand tightly to her chest. Surprisingly though, Mama brought up the subject, "Pauline, I overheard Lindell talking about going to a Can Dance at the high school. I think you should go too—it would be good for you."

Pauline's eyes bulged. "Ya do, Mama? Ya think I should go to the Can Dance?"

"Yes I do, Pauline! Now, I have a dress I can cut down to fit you. I'll have it finished in a day."

"But, Mama, ya know I don't know how to dance."

"Yes, I realize that, Pauline, however, you are a Sampley; you were born with rhythm, and that's all it takes. I've already spoken to Lindell about teaching you a few dance steps."

Pauline threw her head back and rolled her eyes. "Mama, ya didn't!"

"You have nearly a week to learn. Your sister is going, too."

Ohhhhh, as if that will help anything at all! Pauline reflected then quietly said, "Alright, Mama, I guess I might as well go. I know no one will ask me to dance anyway. Guess I don't have to worry—do I?"

"Well, we'll see, Pauline, we'll see," Mama said with a raised eyebrow and a tight grin that quickly changed to a serious frown. "It's about time you had some real fun. You could consider this dance your birthday celebration."

"Can I wear the Lavaliere?"

"Pauline, how many times have we talked about that? You'll wear the Lavaliere for your high school graduation and your wedding, and not a day before!"

* * * * *

Pauline found herself standing on a rickety, wooden chair in the middle of Aunt Julia's kitchen. Her sweaty bare feet seemed to stick to the peeling paint that threatened to poke her as she turned slowly, inch by inch, whenever Mama gave the word.

"Mama, I wish ya wouldn't try to talk with those pins pressed between yer lips—it scares me half to death."

Mama grunted and continued, altering her own familiar faded, yellow frock for Pauline to wear to the dance. Pauline shivered at the worry of one of the pins pricking her waist or midriff. "Pleease be careful, Mama."

"Pauline, if you don't hold still, you will make me stick you!"

At the dinner table that night Mama spoke with determination, "Lindell, maybe you and Pauline should get busy learning those dance steps?"

Pauline quickly searched Lindell's face for any sign of dread or reluctance. When Lindell immediately stood up and lifted one arm into dance position, Pauline blushed, glancing down at the floor.

"So... you're goin', huh, Runt? Well, good fer you! Now, follow me and you'll be just fine—we're gonna move our feet as if we're makin' a box..."

* * * * *

On Friday evening, over dinner, Pauline and the others listened carefully to the men tell about their job search—standing in long lines for hours, only to be turned away, and spending the night alongside the road. Then, finally the long-awaited news; yes, they were hired to pick oranges in Bakersfield. Daddy added sorrowfully, "We'll only be able to come home on weekends though."

There was a unanimous, "Oohhhh noooo."

Pauline whined, "I wish I could pick oranges instead of going to school. At least Delbert gets to work outside! Anyway, Delbert didn't graduate from high school... so why do I have to?"

Mama's back straightened and her complexion flushed. "Pauline, you will attend school so that you'll be able to do something besides pick oranges. If you don't get married right after high school, you'll probably become a seamstress, a waitress, or maybe a cook."

"Mama, ya know that the last place I'd like to work would be a kitchen! I don't have the slightest idea about how to cook anything."

"And that, Pauline, is nobody's fault but your own. God knows I've tried to teach you. It seems your head is always in the clouds when it comes to household chores" — Mama excitingly changed the subject — "Well, you men got home just in time to see the youngin's off to the Can Dance."

Aunt Julia jumped up as if she had sat on a burr. "Sakes alive! Speaking of that, I need to bring a few jars of pickles up from the cellar for the kids to take for the poor folks."

Pauline read the look of unspoken wonder on Daddy and Uncle Charlie's faces — *Why would we be givin' to the poor, when we are the poor?* After a fleeting look between the two men — they remained silent.

"Mama sewed up her old yeller dress fer me too, Daddy."

"Yep, your Mama, she's really somethin' — ain't she?"

Daddy cleared his throat. "Well, well! My Pauline a goin' to her first dance!"

Pauline pivoted around on one heel and crossed the room, planting herself on Daddy's knee. Her arms encircled his shoulders as she whispered into his ear, "I'm really scared, Daddy."

Leaning closer he whispered back, "Hey, my girl will be the belle of the ball, and with the Sampley rhythm ya have nothin' to lose! Jest have fun, honey."

"Oh Daddy, I'll probably just watch anyway..."

Pauline noticed a sympathetic look on Lindell's face. "Tell ya what, Runt, the three of us will ride in the front seat of the truck tonight. Okay?" Pauline smiled, eyes twinkling, but she couldn't answer as a case of nerves had stolen every drop of saliva from her mouth, and her lips fought to slide over the obstacle of her two front teeth.

* * * * *

As the three stepped out of Lindell's truck, Pauline sucked in the enticing sounds of the band warming up. Lindell maneuvered the well-used rope, that was holding the cab door shut, to let himself out of the truck. The others started walking toward the music while Pauline stayed behind scanning the star-filled sky. Then, eyes closed, Pauline inhaled the sweet aroma of wet sagebrush and asphalt after a brief desert rain.

Pauline carefully handed a jar of Aunt Julia's pickles to the school secretary who stood, shoulders erect, next to a box marked "Food for the Poor." Pauline cringed as Lindell disappeared, walking away shoulder to shoulder with two lanky boys, leaving her and June alone in the doorway. June nudged Pauline hard. "For crying out loud, Pauline, breathe. This isn't the end of the world you know. It's supposed to be fun!"

Pauline glared at June. "I'm sick and tired a-hearin' people telling me to have fun." She felt her eyes drawn to the musicians "Let's stand over by the band. Okay, June?"

"Why?"

"Because I want to watch them play."

"Pauline, we didn't come here to watch the band! We came here to dance."

"Not me!"

"Alright, Pauline, but I'm not standing over there all night!"

Two girls waved at June and made their way over. The three talked and giggled while Pauline's eyes drifted to the banjo player, from him to the bass player, and lastly to the guitar player as they warmed up. She watched intently while each plucked the strings of their instrument with a cocked ear. They seemed unaware of the impatient glances of the students.

June's friend, Mary, pointed out that the guitar player was Pearl's pop, the banjo player was Luke's uncle, and the bass player was Herbie's brother. Pauline wished her Daddy were here with his harmonica. She swallowed hard at the thought of being the only one at the dance without a friend.

Suddenly a young woman stepped out in front of the band. She was pretty, with big, blue eyes and thick, curly, brown hair.

"We're going to start the night off with a great Hughie Cannon song: "Bill Bailey, Won't You Please Come Home." Here we go, boys. Ah... one, ah... two, ah... three."

Won't you come home Bill Bailey,
Won't you come home?
She moans the whole day long:
I'll do de cooking, darling, I'll pay de rent;
I knows I've done you wrong."

Pauline stood motionless, mouth agape until the cheers and applause quieted down. "I wanna sing like her someday." Caught up in a world of her own Pauline hadn't noticed the crowd of couples that had gathered on the dance floor.

June's friend, Pearl, suggested they all walk over to the refreshment table where the school principal was serving punch and cookies.

"Hello, Pauline," said Alberta, who had been her reading partner at school earlier that day.

Relieved to have someone call her by name, Pauline hoped her uneasiness didn't show. "Oh, hello, Alberta," she said, "Is this your first dance?"

"Yeah, my first dance."

"Mine, too. Um... thought I was the only one." Although she didn't want to, Pauline knew she was comparing herself to Alberta. *Her hair is kinky, but kinda pretty, never seen anyone with hair so blonde—it's almost white. Can't hardly see her eyelashes—think they're white too. Must be her Ma's shoes—look too big. Wonder how she chipped her front tooth? Yep, guess I like Alberta.*

Alberta hung her head as if trying to escape Pauline's once-over and mumbled, "Have you been asked to dance yet, Pauline?"

"Nope, and I don't care one iota, either." Realizing the rudeness of her obvious critiquing of Alberta's appearance, Pauline added,

"I'll bet you can really cut a rug on the dance floor." It was something she had heard Daddy say to Mama many times, and she thought it must surely be a compliment.

"Well, thanks, Pauline, but I've never danced with a boy before. I sure hope I get asked though."

Pauline noticed June and her friends out on the dance floor. *Guess they aren't havin' any problem?*

"Oh, Pauline, is that dark haired girl your sister?"

"Yah, that's her."

"She is so pretty."

Pauline and Alberta drank punch and ate cookies in silence, brushing crumbs off the collars of their dresses now and then. Their kinship seemed to bring on newfound confidence to both of them.

Alberta mumbled something, her lips barely moving, "Don't look now, but two boys across the room are staring at us." Pauline was suddenly aware of a persistent twitch in left eyelid.

"Just pretend ya don't see them," Pauline whispered while searching for an escape route. Eyes roving she asked, "So, where do ya live, Alberta?"

"Oh, I live close enough to walk to school," she said, running her hand through her hair, then straining to pull up her white socks that had slid down into the heels of her shoes.

"Have you seen the cactus that is shaped like a question mark?"

"Yup, sure have!"

"Well, my house is right there."

"Oh, my, Alberta, those boys are walking this way!" Pauline

quickly turned around toward the wall hoping for a door someplace, but there wasn't one.

Alberta actually started speaking to them! "And this is Pauline", she said.

Finding no way out Pauline responded, "Huh?"

"Pauline, I want you to meet Herbert and Joe."

Arm pressed close to her side, Pauline lifted one finger as she mumbled, "Pleased ta meet ya."

Herbert stood halfway behind Joe, eyes constantly shifting from the floor to the band. Joe stepped a little closer to Alberta. "Would ya like to dance, Alberta?"

Alberta's response was immediate. "Suuurre."

Pauline and Herbert shuffled from one foot to the other while avoiding eye contact. A painful silence followed Herbert's quick glance up at Pauline until she heard a mumbled "Wanna dance?" A warm blush overcame her as she complied with a nervous nod.

* * * * *

Later that night, Pauline rolled her bed out of its bundle that had been propped against the wall. She lay staring up at the ceiling, awaiting any clue that Mama was on her way to bed so she could tell her about the Can Dance.

The sounds of Mama and Aunt Julia laughing and giggling floated across the night air from the main house. Pauline had often watched Mama and Aunt Julia work together as a team, doing laundry, cooking, supervising homework and such, but she couldn't remember Mama ever enjoying herself the way she did on that particular evening. *Um, maybe Mama has missed having the company of a woman she can talk and laugh with.*

When all was quiet, and the only movement was the shadow of Mama's lantern dancing on the walls of the chicken house, Pauline knew Mama was on her way. She lay, chin propped up on her forearms, giggling, as Mama's footsteps quickened to avoid Aunt Julia's ringleader goose, Lucy May, lurking in the shadows, waiting to nip at the back of her ankles.

Life had settled into a routine of sorts. *The stay with Uncle Charlie and Aunt Julia surely has to be a step toward making a living on our own—putting food on the table and having our own roof over our heads.*

Pauline reflected back on their first night spent at the feed house and marveled at Mama's knack for turning any four walls into a home. Before the family had closed their eyes, Mama had rearranged the feed sacks, stacking them against the wall, in order to create a shelf for each one of them. They were expected to keep their clothes neatly folded and stacked on their shelf—shoes set on the floor beneath.

Occasionally, on a cool spring evening, Mama allowed her three youngest to snuggle into bed with her. She piled everyone's covers on top until the weight, and warmth of it all, brought back memories to Pauline of past times spent cuddling with her precious pig, Runt. She could see herself rubbing the soft spot on his forehead and moving down onto his eyelids, and could even remember the sound of his heavy breathing and the smile he aroused with an occasional snort. It was a peace like no other, and it was times like these when the void, created by Daddy and Uncle Charlie being away seemed less noticeable.

* * * * *

One afternoon when the children arrived home from school, Mama, with a glimmer of anticipation in her eyes, sat them down. "Today I walked to town for a few groceries. The desert was alive with wildflowers." Pauline noticed Dale and Lindell beginning to fidget and roll their eyes, but Mama paid no attention and simply continued on—it was the perfect time to pray about the future, which I did while savoring the fragrance of nature."

"As I was opening the screen door at the General Store, I caught sight of a bulletin board with several notices tacked on sort of helter-skelter."

Pauline noticed Lindell's left knee moving up and down impatiently as Mama continued her story—"Two very thin, wrinkled men were leaning against the wall rolling cigarettes, so I went on in, purchased my goods and stopped on the way out to take a close look at that bulletin board."—Pauline cleared her throat to bring Dale and Lindell's attention back to Mama—"I'll tell you, the Lord laid an opportunity right before my eyes. If it had been a snake, it would have bitten me!"

Mama didn't hesitate once, while she rummaged through all corners of her pocketbook until she located a neatly folded piece of paper. The mystery of what lay inside that paper, called her once restless audience to move closer, eyes fixed on Mama as she read:

WANTED
Milker, General Farm Worker, and Cook.
Apply in person.
Pancho Barnes Cattle Ranch.
Family okay.
Includes nice 2 bedroom furnished house.

Mama searched her audience for obvious signs of hope to match her own. Her eyes glistened at the enthusiastic chatter that followed. She slowly raised both hands, then pressed one index finger to her lips to quiet them. "This is why we came to California. I feel it in my bones. How will we ever wait 'til your Daddy gets home on Friday night?"

* * * * *

Sitting on a chair near the front window, Pauline spotted headlights bouncing down the dirt lane to the house. They're here! They're here!" She shouted.

Mama barely allowed time for Daddy to sit down before she retold every detail of her story, ending with the bulletin held firmly against her chest.

Daddy seemed to melt into his chair, a look of youth flowing over his face. "Sounds mighty temptin', Fay, mighty temptin'."

"And, Jack, I could do the cooking."

"Yep, first thing in the morning, we might jest as well take a ride over to this here Pancho Barnes place. Yep, first thing tomorrow morning."

* * * * *

The car trembled as Daddy allowed the tires to roll over a batch of steel pipes covering a shallow trench in the road. Pauline cringed at the clanging and banging of the bald tires on the Oakland tackling the barrier.

"Daddy, what was that anyway?"

"Works jest like a fence, Pauline. Cows are way too skittish to risk comin' close to somethin' so spooky."

"I don't understand, Daddy, there must be hundreds and hundreds of cattle, and you're a-tryin' to tell me that not a one of them will cross through that opening—the only way out? Guess they're a lot like sheep, 'cept they don't have the shepherd to lead them and keep them safe."

Mama shook her head. "Amen, Pauline. I couldn't have said it better myself. And where do we find that story in the Bible?"

"Oh, Mama, look, there's the ranch," Pauline said, changing the subject.

Standing before them was a spread of well-kept outbuildings encircling a large ranch house and one smaller house.

Mama and Daddy stepped out of the car and walked briskly down a path leading to the front door. The remaining three peered out of the car.

After a while, a tall, dark-skinned, and large boned, Pancho Barnes stomped across the heavy planked porch wearing black, high-topped boots. She gave Daddy a firm handshake as she introduced herself.

Mama motioned to Pauline and the others to join them quickly as the woman led the way assertively to a white house with a shingled, peaked roof, and a long porch across the front.

As the rest of the family tumbled out of the car, Pauline gasped, covering her mouth with her hand and whispering, "What! She's a woman?"

June whispered back, "Yes, Pauline. I've heard this is the largest cattle ranch in this part of the country! And it's run by a woman?"

Leading the way Pancho came to an abrupt stop with an outstretched arm, "This is the hired hand's house that goes with the job," she stated nonchalantly in a raspy voice. "You'll get your board, plus wages, in exchange for managing my herd of dairy cows and cooking for my hired hands and me. What do you say, Mr. Sampley?"

"I'd say ya got ya'self a deal, Pancho Barnes, as long as ya don't mind our son joinin' us when he returns from the CCC?"

"We can always use another ranch hand, Mr. Sampley."

When they reached the Oakland, Daddy sat down in the front passenger seat, shutting the door behind them. Mama's jaw dropped open.

"Why, Jack, what in the world are you doing? You know I can't drive."

"Well, Fay, that was yesterday. We need to get back to Charlie's to pick up our belongin's. You might as well learn now."

Chapter Thirteen

On Pauline's 14th birthday, January 1, 1937, the Sampleys crossed the threshold of their new home. Pauline drew in a deep, satisfying breath at the sight of the green painted walls, and an overstuffed sofa and chair, that were camouflaged by green and yellow flowered coverlets. Pauline wondered about a threadbare spot poking out from under a shrunken cover thrown over one of the arms. *Who was here before us? Where were they from? Where have they gone?*

A radio in the far corner of the room caught Pauline's eye. She walked quickly and softly as if she were sneaking into some place she was not allowed. She sat on one of the two wooden chairs on either side of the large, bulky radio. With her eyes closed, Pauline rubbed her cheek against the smooth wood and stroked the cloth-covered speakers, then dreamily glanced into the kitchen.

Four chairs around the table, plus two by the radio. Yes, each member of the Sampley family will have a place of their own.

"Pauline, hurry! Come see our room!"

Running toward the sound of June's voice, Pauline came to a

sudden halt, "Oh June, look!"

A colorful patchwork quilt covered the fluffy, feather bed. A dresser, with an oval mirror centered over the top—and supported by two sets of drawers, almost hid the upholstered dressing stool that had been carefully centered underneath. Pink, sun-bleached curtains hung alongside a window, framing a view of seemingly endless desert dotted with cattle.

The two girls jumped up and down embracing each other. Mama, caught up in their contagious enthusiasm, giggled, and hugged both of them.

Pauline, suddenly serious, turned to Mama, "But, where will the boys sleep?"

"The boys will have the bunkhouse out back, honey."

Arms intertwined, Pauline and June continued hopping about the room. Aware of Mama looking on smiling, Pauline thought she had never seen Mama look younger or prettier.

* * * * *

Once again, the Sampley family gathered at the car ready to unload the remains of their possessions. Each clap of the screen door brought to mind another reminder of the past. Mama's soap kettle; the water bag for the radiator; two wooden crates of clothes; two cooking pots; Daddy's tan hat with the wide black band; Mama's Treasure Chest with the Bible and Lavaliere. Pauline felt she would explode from the excitement welling up inside her.

Pauline hollered, "Where do ya want the bedrolls, Mama?" She said with a deep sigh. *Yes! We have real beds now!*

"Take them out to the bunkhouse, sweetheart. You never know when we might need them again."

We'll never need those bedrolls again! I'm as sure as sure can be.

A door slamming off in the distance caught Pauline's attention. Pancho was heading toward them holding a kettle with a thick dish-towel covering the wire handle. Pauline and Dale watched from behind the screen door while the others greeted her.

Pancho's voice was low and gruff, "Thought you folks might make use of this here pot of beans."

"Thank you kindly, Miss Barnes," said Daddy, reaching for the steaming kettle. "Folks around here call me Pancho," the woman said disinterestedly.

Pauline strained to hear Mama's whisper-soft voice.

"Um... Pancho, this is such a nice place to live. The house is so homey. I can't imagine why anyone would ever want to leave it..."

Pancho's thoughts seemed to wander off. Then, her dark, penetrating eyes snapped back toward Mama. "Yes, the O'Hara family, they left rather suddenly... Fay, you'll have breakfast ready for twelve hired hands by six in the morning, seven days a week. Keep in mind that my bedroom is next to the kitchen—I'd appreciate a little quiet.

'Jack, the milking begins at four-thirty in the morning. Oh, and another thing, I'm assuming the younger children will continue their schooling?" Pancho waited with one eyebrow cocked, but before Mama had a chance to speak, she continued. "The school bus stops out on the highway around seven-thirty in the morning."

As Pancho turned to leave, Pauline's mouth dropped at the sight of her long, thick, black braid tapping the worn leather belt looped through her khaki work pants. It seemed to be keeping time with the striding gait of Pancho's brown, leather boots.

❋ ❋ ❋ ❋ ❋

Pauline lay next to June, looking out the window at the stars reflecting the light of a full moon. Encased by their thick feather mattress and the lull of June's heavy breathing, Pauline retraced her day—neatly stacking six mismatched plates next to six odd sized fruit jars that served as drink glasses, on the cupboard shelf; Pancho and her mysterious comment about the O'Hara's; eating dinner together as a family and sitting on real chairs; in the evening, and Daddy turning on the news and the radio blaring.

Pauline, June, and Dale huddled around the radio, harmonizing to the song, "I've Got a Pocket Full of Dreams." June, sitting on one end of the sofa with a book on her lap; Mama at the other end, mending Daddy's coveralls; Daddy in the overstuffed chair just listening to everyone sing; and then Mama's Bible reading, *But let patience have her perfect work, that ye may be perfect and entire, wanting nothing...*

"Amen," Pauline whispered to herself.

❋ ❋ ❋ ❋ ❋

Pauline spotted a figure walking toward them, coming from the direction of the small town she remembered passing through the day before. As the figure grew closer, Mama gasped, raising the back of her hand to her mouth. Realizing it was Delbert; the children took off running across the desert. Squealing, they all wrapped their arms around him excitedly, and led him to the door where Mama and Daddy stood motionless. Mama rocked

Delbert back and forth while Daddy just smiled, eyes moist.

Delbert talked late into the night about his experiences over the past six months, "It wasn't bad, I stayed in the labor camp's housing with about two hundred young men like myself. One of my assignments was to fight fires. I did forest restoration and road construction too. I learned a lot, and I think I grew up a lot, too, but I'm sure happy to be back with my family." His face brightened as he reached into his pant pocket and handed his wages over to Daddy. Daddy swallowed hard as tears ran down his cheeks.

Delbert shrugged his shoulders. "Just finished a job nearby and thought I might as well join back up with my folks again since we're all in California now."

Mama held Delbert tightly. "That's right son, we're on our way now, aren't we?"

* * * * *

Mama's three youngest stood at the edge of the road as she drove back home and out of sight. Even though she sat on a pillow, the top of her head was barely visible through the back window of the car. They watched the car lunge and sputter until it disappeared out of sight.

Pauline shaded her eyes with the flat of her hand while squinting into the sun in search of the school bus. "Think I'll be taller than Mama when I grow up, June?"

June replied curtly, "Not at the rate you're going!"

The sky was bright blue, bulging with disfigured clouds. Pauline slid one foot side-to-side in the loose, grainy sand with eyes skyward and her neck awkwardly contorted. "Hey, that cloud looks like a pig," she exclaimed, but her attempt to get June and Dale interested was to no avail. They seemed too caught up in their own preoccupation with what was to come.

Pauline saw something move under a raggedy sage bush. Leaning over and reaching way under the rough branches, she pulled a lizard out by the tail, studying it as it squirmed and wiggled. She giggled as June and Dale stepped aside.

"Why do ya think Pancho acted so funny 'bout that O'Hara family?"

Pauline noticed June's jaw tighten. "Pauline, it's none of our business!"

Dale, looking up at the two of them thoughtfully suggested, "Maybe our house is haunted. Maybe a ghost got 'em."

"They probably wanted to move to the city," said June. "Like anyone with an ounce of sense."

Pauline glanced off down the highway. "Oh no, Lord be with us, here comes the school bus."

A dull looking truck, with a tarp stretched over the truck bed, rolled to a stop in front of them.

* * * * *

At supper that evening, Pauline relished sharing the day's events. Stories of Delbert getting "cow kicked" because he was too stubborn to listen—Daddy had told him he needed to lean into the hind quarter of the cow to prevent the bruises that he now proudly flaunted—and Mama's stories of Pancho herding cattle like a man—working harder than any man she had ever known.

Taking advantage of the jovial mood in the air, Delbert waddled bowlegged across the kitchen floor—chin high, and chest puffed, thumbs hooked over the front pockets of his Levis. He spoke with an exaggerated twang. "The ranch hands asked me to go to town with them tonight."

The jovial mood was cut short though as Mama drew in a deep breath, folded her arms across her chest, and leaned back in her rocker. "Going to town, to do what?" She asked.

"He'll be okay, Fay, that's jest part of becoming a man."

Mama's frown was accompanied by a faint growl.

June broke the tense silence that followed. "I have good news. I have a new friend in my class; her name is Margaret."

Pauline flashed a longing glance in June's direction. Quickly overcoming her twinge of jealousy, she announced, "I have good news, too. I wasn't the first to sit down in the Spelling Bee. Ya must be a pretty good teacher, Mama!" She said grinning.

While Delbert gathered his hat and coat, Pauline strained to hear their words as he and Daddy stood shoulder to shoulder near the door, their backs to the rest of the family. "Here's two bits, son. Ya might need a little spendin' money."

Pauline spotted Mama eyeing them suspiciously.

Chapter Fourteen

The remaining four weeks of school passed slowly before the long-awaited thrill of the last day. As the bus dropped them off in the afternoon, Pauline, June, and Dale lay their school mementos down on the warm, tightly packed dirt road. They waved enthusiastically at the sight of the family car jerking and jiggling toward them on the unevenness of its path. Dry heat rose in heavy waves.

The three watched—feet burning through the soles of their shoes—Mama approached, clutching the steering wheel and straining to make a U-turn on the deserted road. The squealing brakes seemed to announce the start of summer vacation.

Grabbing the Oakland's front door handle, Pauline loudly proclaimed, "It's my turn to sit in the front!" She jumped in and leaned her head back against the stiff, velvety upholstery, smirking happily. "The whole summer off," she whispered to herself.

June, interrupting Pauline's tranquility, giggled and teased while questioning, "Hello, is anybody up there? I can't see anyone sitting in the front seat!"

Pauline felt her jaw tighten. Knitting her reddish-blonde eyebrows together up over the bridge of her nose, she whined, "Mama, jest 'cause I told June I wished I was tall, now she's a teasin' me 'bout bein' short, and you too, Mama, fer that matter."

"It's frustrating when things we say come back to bite us, isn't it, Pauline? Especially when we trusted the person we confided in." Mama started humming "What Friend We Have in Jesus," which meant that the conversation was over.

June mumbled in a barely audible voice, "Sorry, Pauline."

Mama appeared caught up in her own thoughts before blurting out, "I'll tell you one thing, Pauline. We're going to make good use of this summer vacation from school to work on your grammar. Your Daddy and I will not have any of our children talking like dumb Okies."

"Mama!"

"Pauline, believe me when I say, it will be over my dead body."

* * * * *

In the kitchen, Pauline boosted herself onto the fractured linoleum-covered countertop and sat facing Mama. "Mama, have ya noticed that old cemetery—way out south of Pancho's place?" Pauline absentmindedly spun the pan of Mama's warm Angel Food cake. The pan wobbled precariously on top of a long-necked cough syrup bottle so it would cool faster.

"Leave that cake alone before you cause it to fall!" Mama protested. Adhering to Mama's warning, Pauline placed her folded hands on her lap and continued spilling her thoughts.

"Well, Mama, if ya walk out behind Pancho's house and look

straight south, you'll see the top half of a wooden cross. Think maybe tomorrow Dale, and I will go looking around."

"Pauline, if you don't take all," Mama said rolling her eyes and shaking her head.

* * * * *

In the cool of the evening, supper was taken out on the porch. Delbert turned the radio volume up, and when the hit song "Beer Barrel Polka" came on the air, Pauline and June couldn't resist dancing. Holding hands, they twirled around and around on the front porch, then down the steps, and onto the lawn.

Ranch hands, Butch and Scotty, were walking along the footpath leading to the side door of Pancho's. Butch, taking hold of one of the tightly rolled sides of his hat, tipped it slightly toward June. He glanced shyly at the rest of the clan. "Howdy, Sampleys. Sure could use some rain." He tipped his hat again — "Howdy, June."

Pauline gulped, turning to June just in time to see a red flush washing over her china doll complexion. Daddy seemed obviously shaken by the attention paid to his firstborn daughter. As the men disappeared he chose his words carefully, "These young cowboys 'round here don't see many pretty, young girls. Not real young ladies, like mine. Ya can be polite, but other than that, ya needn't pay them no never mind, ya hear?"

June blushed again, while Pauline simply wondered, *Is Daddy talking to me, too?*

Pauline and June replied simultaneously, "Yes, Daddy."

* * * * *

The light of day was barely visible when Mama rang the huge cast iron bell calling the ranch hands to breakfast. It was the signal for Pauline and June to make sure their early morning chores were done and get over to Pancho's kitchen to help Mama clean up.

The men were just getting up from the table. Pauline caught sight of a few glances in June's direction. Irritated, she cupped her hands around both eyes and stared back. June's elbow caught her in the ribs. "Act your age, Pauline!"

Mama washed the dishes. The girls dried. Bored, Pauline was just beginning to get some enthusiasm for the second verse of "Stormy Weather" when Pancho hollered, "Would it be possible for a gal to get some sleep around here?" Startled, Mama held her chest, throwing her head back and rolling her eyes toward the ceiling. "Sorry, Pancho."

"She's mean," Pauline said in a low whisper. "We're jest singin'."

"It's 'just singing,'" said Mama.

Later, Pauline located Dale in the big barn. "Wanna go look at that ol' cemetery, Dale?"

"Sure. I'll have to ask Daddy if he is done with me fer while."

Standing on tiptoes, Dale stretched up, looking for Daddy where he had been stacking hay in the loft. "Daddy, can I go with Pauline fer awhile?"

"Long as yer back by lunch, so ya Mama won't worry."

The two set off walking, shoulder to shoulder, heads down, kicking a rock back and forth between them.

"Think it'll be spooky, Pauline?"

"Naw, just stay close to me."

The two zigzagged between what was left of the weathered grave markers. They slowed as they neared one headstone—the epitaph nearly worn away. On his knees, Dale traced the roughly engraved marker with his finger, while Pauline strained to read the words:

GRACE AND BABY MARIE O'HARA
FATHER FORGIVE HER
1921-1937

The two stared at the stone in a silence, disturbed only by their own rapid breathing. Finally, they looked at each other through wondering eyes. Pauline questioned aloud—asking no one and expecting no answer, "Father, forgive her for what?"

"Dale, she was only 16 years old. What could she have done?"

"Pauline, remember when you was a pickin' cotton that time and you pretended you couldn't hear Mama's arithmetic problems, cause you was lazy?"

"I was not lazy, Dale. I was just hot and sweaty and didn't want to!"

"Well, Mama did say she forgave you though, didn't she?"

"Yes, she sure did, Dale. This though—this is bad!"

They were almost home before either spoke. "Dale, maybe we shouldn't have gone up there. Maybe some things is jest better left alone. Mama and Daddy have been so happy—we wouldn't want to muddy the waters. Oh, poor Dale, ya probably don't even know what that means, do ya?"

"Aw, come on, Pauline, I wanna tell 'bout the O'Hara's to the others back at the ranch..."

"Dale, do ya remember the other night when Mama was a readin' to us from the Bible? Ya remember when she read 'bout the ships that be so great, and are driven by strong winds, yet can be turned about with a very small—rudder? Later, I asked Mama what that meant, and she said that the ship is like us, big and strong. Our tongue is like the rudder of our bodies. The words that roll off our tongue can change our whole direction, our whole life. Do ya want your life to change, Dale? Do ya?"

* * * * *

Pauline and Dale focused earnestly on each bite of their supper. Thinking that their aloofness had gone unnoticed, Pauline was startled when Daddy suddenly turned to her, asking, "So, what did you and Dale do today?" Pauline quickly replied before Dale had a chance to open his mouth, "Ohhh, we just walked out south of Pancho's and back."

To Pauline's relief, Daddy changed the subject. "Talked to ol' Jake today—ya know, Pancho's longtime ranch boss? Yep, that Jake is a real nice fella. Gonna be eighty-five next week. Thought maybe we could have him in fer dinner. Huh, Fay?"

* * * * *

Jake was early. Daddy groaned while pulling himself up out of his chair—twisting his back from side to side. One corner of the screen door produced an ear-piercing scraping noise as he pushed it open. "Good to see ya, Jake," Daddy said extending his hand. "I was jest listening to the news. Did ya hear about that Douglas DC-4E that flew all the way from Chicago to New York—fifty-two passengers! Who woulda thought it could be done?"

Jake nodded. "Umm, umm—in this day and age, too. June 7th, 1938—Umm, umm!"

Eavesdropping from the kitchen was not enough to satisfy Pauline's curiosity about their first, non-family visitor. She stood half concealed by the doorway of the kitchen, shyly watching, as Jake nodded with amazement at Daddy's news. It seemed that his tanned, wrinkled skin would slide right off his face were it not for a full head of white hair and a thick, matching mustache holding it in place.

Jake strained to catch a glimpse of Pauline and, when his eyes settled on her, he asked, "And who have we here, Jack? Who's this girl with the pretty red hair and freckles?"

Pauline shuddered. *Why, oh why, does everyone have to mention my red hair and freckles before they even know me?*

"Come on in, Pauline," Daddy said. "Come in and meet Jake."

With short hesitating steps, Pauline crossed the floor to Daddy's side. "Hello Jake, I've seen ya takin' ya meals over at Pancho's."

"Dinner is served," said Mama in such a polished manner that everyone, except Jake, stood motionless for a time wondering what Mama expected them to do. Jake quickly made his way to the kitchen, continuing to talk while he perched himself on the first chair he came to—the one with the back broken off. He didn't seem to notice.

"I'm most obliged to ya fer the invite, Mrs. Sampley. If ya only knew how long it's been since I've had a real home-cooked meal. The good Lord himself must surely be a burstin' with pride at the kind of hospitality y'all are a heapin' on me. Course, far be it from me to suggest that the good Lord be a prideful soul."

He removed his hat, folded his dry wrinkled hands together, and bowed his head for the blessing of the meal.

By the time Mama's chicken and dumplings were gone, Pauline was surprised at how well Jake fit into the family. The conversation between Jake and Daddy freely flowed. They spoke of Roosevelt extending the Social Security Act to include women and children; the adoption of the first local food stamp program being tried in New York City and that it would make people too dependent on the Government; of a car going 125 miles an hour at a race in Indianapolis, and the winner drinking milk.

When the conversation turned less serious, Pauline spoke hesitantly, "So, Jake... has Pancho ever been married?"

"Oh, she's been married... Fact is, her husband owned this place—was passed down to him from his folks. I heard tell they was well-to-do. Should have been clear as a bell to him beforehand that Pancho was a long way from prim and proper.

"Guess it's true what they say, love is blind. Anyways, Pancho definitely had a mind of her own and made no bones about it. To be honest with ya, I was mighty skeptical 'bout the future of this place, even in the best of times with him a runnin' things. Yep, William Barnes would have squandered every penny he ever made if it weren't fer Pancho.

"There's somethin' 'bout that woman. When she sets her mind to somethin', there ain't nothin' gonna change it. Does the work of two men she will—out there on the range roundin' up them cattle in all kinds of weather—rain a peltin', sand a blowin', or sun a burnin'. Never met another like 'er.

"Course, when the Depression hit there wasn't much anyone could do. One day, William Barnes himself jest up and walked out. Weren't long 'fore Pancho let all the cowboys go, 'cept fer me and young Billy.

"Ya, Billy was sixteen years old when I first met him. Sure rough around the edges he was. Father was a drunkard. Wouldn't be proper to discuss his mother in the presence of children.

"Billy started gettin' in trouble with the law, ya know—jest little things. He lifted a pack of cigarettes from the store over in town. Spent one day a drivin' all over tarnation in Pancho's truck— knew he'd get caught.

"Didn't seem to care after a while. Sheriff felt sorry fer him he did. Brought him to me. Lord knows why... thought maybe I'd get him straightened out I guess, 'fore it was too late."

Pauline took advantage of a lull in the conversation. "Ya must have known the O'Hara's—the family who lived here before us?"

"The O'Haras? Ah yes, I knew 'em well," he said, leaning back in his chair while stuffing his pipe with tobacco that he carefully plucked from a worn pouch. "Eliz'beth O'Hara was Pancho's sister. Course you'd never have know'd they was sisters, not in a million years. Eliz'beth O'Hara was as straight-laced as they come. And how she watched over those youngin's was like a mother hen a watchin' over her chicks.

"Eliz'beth's husband, Michael, was strict 'bout keepin' his family together. If he'd sent those boys off to the CCC work program they could have helped put bread on the table as well as maybe learn a trade... but I ain't never had no kids of my own, so who am I to judge?

"The only kid I'd ever been around was Billy. I think the only thing that boy ever wanted was a real family. Could kinda see the writin' on the wall, I could. Oh, I tried to talk to him, but he seemed in awe of the whole O'Hara family, especially Grace Marie.

"As time wore on, it 'came clear that Grace was with child. Parents aged overnight they did. Sent Billy on his way. Never saw him again!

"Was late one cold winter's night—I was a sittin' at the window rolling a cigarette when I noticed their lights on—I figured it was Grace's time. Couldn't sleep much after that, so jest sat there, a lookin' out, a wonderin'. Saw one of the O'Hara's younger girls runnin' fast toward Pancho's back door.

"Spotted Michael a headin' fer my place, so I met him halfway. He looked like death itself.

Both Grace and the baby passed that night. Eliz'beth never was right after that. She died a year later. I say it was a broken heart?"

Chapter Fifteen

Pauline hated the look in Mama's eyes—it was all too familiar.
She remembered seeing that look once before. It was the day
the Fed's showed up at the soddy. That faraway stare, the heavy
creases across the bridge of her nose, the wringing of her hands—
alternating one on top of the other.

As Pauline peered into the living room, she could tell Mama and
Daddy were talking serious. She pushed her chair back out of
sight and pressed her ear against the wall.

"Jack, those ladies that have been coming around Pancho's just
don't look right to me. Makes me feel uncomfortable serving
them breakfast in the mornings. They're painted up and have a
sort of irritating, flirty giggle. I have a strong feeling things are
taking a turn for the worst.

"I don't like our girls being around such goings-on! Those ladies,
if you can call them that, hanging all over the men and all! What
do you make of it, Jack?"

"Well Fay, there's something else too. The ranch hands 'round
here are startin' to look at our girls in a different way. I don't like

what I'm a seein'. In fact, I won't have it! It's not only the girls we have to think about, but it's our sons too. What kind of an example is it fer them?"

"Jack, we've been so happy here. I'd never have imagined this kind of a cloud coming over us."

Pauline's neck was beginning to ache and her ear was feeling hot and numb from pressing it so hard against the wall. She closed her eyes and through gritted teeth imagined yelling, *No, no, no,* way down deep in her gut where no one could hear. *Pancho's is perfect for us.*

She picked up where she had left off, hunched over, ear pressed hard against the wall.

"Alright, Fay, I'll agree to a one week trial, but no longer. We can't leave the lives of our children to chance—they're too precious to us—even if it means having to leave this here paradise on earth."

Pauline imagined Mama beginning to twiddle her thumbs nervously. "Jack, I agree with you, and I am so very relieved that we have a plan. I think this has been weighing heavily on both of us." Pauline didn't see, but they held each other tightly. Mama prayed sorrowfully, "Lord, may our eyes be opened to your holy guidance."

* * * * *

Pauline slowly turned the knob on the kerosene lamp to lower the wick, then bending over, she blew out the flame. She stretched across the bed, turning toward June. "Pssssst."

"For goodness sake, what is it, Pauline?"

"I overheard Mama and Daddy talking today."

"So?"

"So... they were talking 'bout leaving the ranch. They think there's something strange going on here and that Pancho is some kind of a ringleader or something. They don't want us to turn' out bein' like those painted ladies hangin' around the cowboys. But, shoot, June, truth is, I'd give my lucky stars to look like any one of them."

"Pauline, don't you ever say that again! Do you hear me?

"June, what are ya so upset about? What's so bad about them anyway?"

"Pauline, have you had your head stuck in the sand all of your life? Those women could be Ladies of the Night! Do you know anything about the world at all?

Do you remember the time Mama got after me for reading that magazine she called a love magazine?"

"Yeah, Mama was really sore at you. "

"Yes, she was Pauline. That's because you and I shouldn't be filling our heads with such things. Mama says that the Bible tells us to fill our heads only with things that are lovely and pure."

"I realize it was wrong, but truth be told, that's where I learned about Ladies of the Night, Pauline. No... you don't want to be like any of those women!"

* * * * *

Pauline awoke at the first hint of Mama getting ready for work.

"Pauline, what are you doing up so early — why, you're all dressed!"

"Oh, Mama, I thought I would go to work with ya to help ya out a little this morning. Thought maybe I could help ya serve. Cut down on ya havin' to carry all those heavy trays by yer self."

"I don't think so Pauline, it's not a good place for you to be hanging around."

"But Mama, how am I ever going to learn anything about the world if all you and Daddy do is protect me from it?"

"Oh Pauline! Ask your father—whatever he says goes!"

"Daddy, can I go to work with Mama this morning if I stay right with her, helping her carry the heavy trays and such?"

Daddy looked at Pauline sternly, "Well, okay, but ya stay right near ya Mama—hear?"

"Thanks, Daddy."

As the twosome walked the well-worn path to the grub house, Pauline noticed for the first time that she was now as tall as Mama. The early morning sun was already intense, and the scents of hay, cow manure, and the fine dust stirred up by their shoes seemed sweetly familiar.

Pauline's selfish motive of helping Mama, only to take a closer look at the Ladies of the Night had faded. She now sensed that Mama was impressed, if not somewhat puzzled, at her eagerness to help.

In her mind, Pauline pictured her eyes scanning those in the grub house. She knew she would make a decision about right and wrong today, and that this decision would help her understand what the older family members must have seen—that she somehow had missed.

The wood-sided screen door leading to the kitchen stood slightly ajar and banged lightly against the frame with each puff of the light, desert wind. Opening the door for Mama, Pauline thought unhappily, that nothing was ever as perfect as it seemed.

Mama started working as soon as she stepped onto the worn linoleum kitchen floor. She went to a green painted cupboard and, standing on her toes, reached for a large mixing bowl from the top cupboard shelf.

"Want me to get that for you," Pauline said trying to speak correctly using a more mature voice.

"Not necessary... Pauline! Thank you, anyway. I do this most every day." Pauline watched as Mama carefully scooted the bowl toward her with a wooden spoon until she tilted it causing it to tip into her awaiting hand."

Pauline found herself cringing at the sight—imagining the bowl to end up landing squarely in the middle of Mama's forehead. *She is soooo stubborn.*

Without turning around Mama chanted, "Pauline, run to the hen house for eggs while I start the biscuits."

Pauline readily obeyed, not wanting to push her luck. When she breathlessly returned with a basket of eggs, Mama was sifting flour into the bowl.

"Now, get a glass from the cupboard, dip the rim into this plate of flour, and cut out some biscuits. Grease that baking sheet with some lard from that jar there in the corner, and place the rounds on the baking sheet—about an inch apart.

Holding her tongue to one side, Pauline diligently pressed through the fluffy white dough and then gave the glass a tap, releasing each round with a plop. The two didn't talk, but instead became engrossed in their work. After the last biscuit, Pauline fanned a puff of rising flour dust away from her nose. Her voice was hoarse from inhaling the fine powder, "Mama, can I set the table?"

"Sure, Pauline, that will be fine... but when the cowboys start coming in, I want you back in this kitchen. Do you hear me?"

"I hear, Mama, I hear."

Pauline worked ceremoniously until startled by the sound of a door flying open and guys and gals laughing. She quickly glanced over at the kitchen pass through, wondering if Mama was watching.

The sounds coming from the kitchen told her that Mama was working at full speed and had possibly forgotten her own advice. Pauline turned her attention back to her undertaking and, sure enough, a gal with blonde hair was ambling over toward one of the ranch hands.

The two seemed to be whispering some secrets and then the woman threw her head back with a loud shrieking laugh, revealing a smudge of red lipstick across one tooth. When she stopped laughing, Pauline stared at the bright red lipstick that had filled the deep wrinkles lining her lips. She studied the makeup the woman wore. A thick black line accentuated the crevices at the corners of her eyes. Red rouge exaggerated her high cheekbones. The collar of her white blouse was stained with beige makeup.

Pauline felt a sense of nausea and an unexplainable fear coming over her.

The door opened again, and two more gals walked in. They seemed to know everyone there. Pauline was suddenly aware that Mama was scowling at her. She took that as a sign that she needed to get to the kitchen right away.

Pauline burst through the wooden swinging doors. Her arms were crossed tightly across her chest. She took deep, rapid breaths.

"Oh, Mama! I think I'm going to be sick."

"Pauline! What did I tell you about staying back here with me?"

"Mama, I had to see fer myself. If you and Daddy pulled us away from the first place we've loved in a long time... well, I'm not sure I could have forgiven you if I hadn't seen fer myself."

"Well, did you, Pauline? Did you see for yourself?"

"Yes. Mama, we can't stay here at Pancho's place anymore, can we?"

"No Pauline...we can't. But, we'll wait out the rest of the week before we talk about it as a family. Now, don't worry your pretty head honey, God will take care of us Sampleys."

* * * * *

Pauline stepped gingerly off of the front porch while watching a slowly approaching car. She squinted into the sun, puzzled by the oncoming stranger.

The car door opened and out stepped a shiny black and white leather shoe topped by a tightly creased pant leg reaching for the running board of the car. The man was tall, with a straight, proud back and dark, wavy hair. *He looks like a movie star.*

"Well, hello," he said. "I'll bet Mr. Sampley is your Daddy?"

"Yup! He's out in the barn. Follow me, and I'll show you. Or, maybe you'd rather drive... it's kinda a dusty walk?"

"I've always said, a little dirt builds a lot of character," said the handsome gentleman.

Surprised by his statement, Pauline looked up into his eyes as if some unspoken language would tell her more about the stranger.

Daddy was pitching hay onto a flat-bed wagon when Pauline called to him from the barn door. Pitchfork in hand, he dabbed at the sweat dripping down his face with the back of his shirtsleeve, leaving traces of straw and dirt stuck to his forehead.

The outsider in the tweed sports coat and white starched shirt looked out of place standing next to Daddy in his bib overalls and wide-brimmed straw hat. Pauline backed away, hoisting herself up and sitting cross-legged on a couple of hay bales.

Hmmm... I'd forgotten the sound of Daddy's slow easy drawl and the deep chuckle that starts at his belly and work its way up to his cheeks where it pushes all the wrinkles up to the corners of his eyes. Daddy likes him. She recalled a vivid picture in her mind— of Daddy and Uncle Charlie sitting on overturned buckets out by the windmill with the sun setting.

Pauline's thoughts were broken when June appeared carrying a jug of water and two glasses on a tray. Pauline grinned, knowing that her unsuspecting sister was about to be caught off guard. As June approached Daddy and the stranger, Pauline noticed June nervously running her fingers through her hair.

Daddy proudly introduced his eldest daughter. "Oh, June, this here's Charles Jones Jr. He's jest tryin' to land himself some extra work 'round these parts."

June tugged at the waistline of her dress while stiffly extending her hand. Charles took her hand softly, seeming to hold on longer than she expected, triggering red blotches to quickly creep up her chest and neck.

Pauline thought he looked more like he was going to kiss her hand than shake it.

As if dutifully awaiting the task of returning the pitcher, June boosted herself up next to Pauline. She sat tall and proper—legs crossed at the knees—seemingly focused on the view outside the barn, unconcerned about the conversation between Daddy and Charles.

Eventually, Daddy seemed to sense that Charles needed to get back on the road. As June reached over to take Charles' glass, Pauline noticed a moment of delayed lingering. Charles asked, "May I give you a hand with that tray, June?"

Daddy spoke up immediately, "Oh, she'll be fine."

When June started back to the house, Pauline scampered along behind her. They both burst into the kitchen where Mama was peeling potatoes. June stood behind Mama with her fists clenched tight and her body tense. "Mama, I just can't believe that you and Pauline could have been so dreadfully thoughtless as to allow me to make such an appearance with no warning at all! I don't suppose either of you is capable of understanding why it would possibly matter to me that I was completely unprepared to meet the most handsome and polite man on the face of the earth—Who, by the way, will never, ever, care if he lays eyes on me again!"

Pauline threw her hands up in the air, "Well, Mama told you to take two glasses June, now why would she do that if there weren't two people out there? Huh? Huh?"

Pauline stared down at the floor under raised eyebrows—lips pressed firmly together.

Mama passed the potato peeler to June without looking up. "June, make yourself useful. Peel these potatoes while I rest my feet awhile."

Pauline struggled to keep from snickering while glancing over at Mama—who was, cleverly, bent over rubbing her swollen ankles while stifling a case of the giggles.

Mama spoke casually, "So, what's his name, dear?"

"Charles, Mama. His name is Charles Robert Jones Junior," replied June, as she reached for a paring knife to quarter the potatoes.

Pauline dramatically jumped back. "Hey, June, watch it—you could have cut me!"

"Oh, I am so sorry—how could I have been so careless!"

"Girls, that's enough!" shouted Mama.

Sitting upright now, the obvious sincerity in Mama's eyes was calming. "So, June, just what's so special about this Mr. Charles Robert Jones Junior?"

Seeming to take this as a cue to put down her knife and pull up a chair, June looked past Pauline as if she were invisible. Her complexion turned pink and her eyes seemed almost blue-black as she spoke directly to Mama. "Mama, he is so handsome. His hair is thick, wavy and nearly black. He's tall and had on a sport-coat, tie, pleated pants and black and white leather shoes. Daddy and Charles were talking in the barn. He said he'd gone to an all-boys college for two years."

Mama looked puzzled. "What brings such a fellow to these parts, for goodness sake?"

"He told Daddy that when The Depression caused his family to split up, his Aunt took him in. She put him through college.

"Now, he works at the Golden Queen Mine in Mojave and lives with his Uncle Amos. He was hoping he could take on a second job working here at the dairy barn. He's real good at sports, too! He even picks up a few extra dollars boxing on Saturday nights."

Mama frowned at the thought. "Boxing? Only the town hooligans go to those boxing matches, but I guess he's at least trying to make a living during these hard times. Guess I can't wrong him for that, and he does live with his Uncle—not just out on his own in some boarding house or something."

At the sound of a car engine starting up, June ran to the window. "Well, there he goes. Guess that's the last time I'll see him."

At dinner that night June brought up the subject. "So, Daddy, were you able to offer Charles any work?"

"Charles who?"

"Charles Robert Jones Junior, from Mojave, Daddy, for goodness sake, who else?"

"Oh him... nope... couldn't! Told him he's too nice a guy to be workin' here. And now that ya bought it up, June, ya Mama and I have decided to pull up stakes. Yep, we're pullin' out on Monday morning."

Daddy winked at June, "I believe we'll head out toward Mojave, matter of fact." June's whimpering came to a sudden halt.

"Yep, this here place feeds our bellies and our pride, but sure ain't doin' nothing fer our souls."

That night Mama chose her scripture by reading wherever the pages of the Bible parted. "Proverbs 4:11. *I have taught thee in the way of wisdom; I have led thee in right paths.*"

Why is it that these readings always seem that they've been hand-picked just fer us?

In the quiet that followed, Pauline asked with a quivering voice, "Mama, may I see the Lavaliere?"

Mama's fingertips searched the bottom of the velvet-lined chest from memory. Cradling the Lavaliere in both hands—she placed it on Pauline's palm.

"Remember, Pauline, you girls will wear this when you graduate from high school and on your wedding days."

"Mama, I'm not sure I will ever get to wear the Lavaliere."

"Why do you say that, Pauline?"

"Because I don't think I will ever finish high school. And I never want to get married, because I never want to leave you and Daddy."

Mama held her hand out for the Lavaliere and laid it back in the chest. "Yes, Pauline, you'll wear the Lavaliere someday, I promise..."

Chapter Sixteen

Leaning out the window of the Oakland, Pauline rested her chin on her scrawny forearm. With a sigh, she watched Daddy and Mama walk into Pancho's kitchen for the last time. *The pay we get today will have to last 'til—who knows when,* she thought. *I hate Pancho Barnes and her stupid house.* She turned away, allowing her eyes to roam what was left of the desert oasis she had loved... for a time.

In her mind, she traced the silhouette of the main house, the barn, the bunkhouse, the springhouse, and the windmill... all soon to be memories past. Her eyes rested on the whitewashed picket fence, gray wood already showing through the once chalk-white slats.

I remember the day Mama asked Dale and me to paint that fence. Couldn't believe she thought we could handle a job like that? Seemed more like play, at first, but as the sun climbed higher, sweat drowned out all signs of laughter and brotherly love. Hot words had floated to the surface.

You're slower than molasses in January.

Well, you're sloppy as an ol' pig.

Mama's gonna be mad.

I'm tellin'.

But, on this day, the sloping front porch of the house stood bare, no scattered mismatched chairs up for grabs. Pauline longed for even a hint of the late night conversation, laughter, music, and dancing that the porch knew. Instead, it appeared ghostly.

As Daddy pulled the car around, Pauline squinted hard through streaks of shadows and sunlight for one last look inside the barn. She startled everyone as she shouted, "Hey, there's somebody in there already." Then her voice trailed off, "Out early today I guess."

June shot Pauline a perturbed glare, "Keep your voice down, you don't have to shout."

"Ah, it's Hank and Willie," Pauline whispered fondly while spinning around on her knees—pressing her forehead against the back window. *Never knew why they rolled their hat brims up so tight on the sides like that.* Spotting the end of a rope flapping in the breeze on Mama's side of the car, Daddy got out to "secure things up top."

Thank you, Lord, for letting him stop right here, in front of the barn. Pauline seemed captivated by the seesaw rhythm of the two cowboys working together as they loaded hay.

She remembered days past—dangling her bare feet over the edge of the loft—the dry, prickly hay sticking and poking the backs of her legs. She hated the itchy red rash that Mama was always eager to rub with vinegar. Eyes closed tight, she imagined the sweet-sour scent of the barn and straw kneaded with cow dung by careless hooves.

Pauline sought to etch the whole scene into her mind. To stow it away—should a case of the blues unexpectedly come over her down the road apiece. *Sorta like the year I started kindergarten—I truly needed to continually rub Mama's pink satin slip across my cheek and my right eyelid before drifting off to sleep each night.* She remembered her surprise when Mama cut the slinky under-garment into squares that eventually became thin, frayed, and honeycombed with holes. Why would Mama ever do such a thing? Mama never had anything beautiful, except for that pink slip, and the Lavaliere, of course.

Don't know why I'm a feelin' this way. I know full well that leavin' Pancho is right. Guess I'm scared of what the future holds. Shouldn't be!

Off in the distance, white-faced cattle roamed freely, moving in clusters from one scattered patch of yesterday's hay allotment to another. *Like something interesting is about to occur in their otherwise boring lives.*

By the time they neared the sun-bleached board fence, separated only by a cattle guard, the heifers had stopped their obsessive chewing and stood shoulder to shoulder, staring, maybe daring the Sampley's to turn around. Go back.

Why do cows always have to stare... must be dumb, 'fraid to walk cross a bunch of steel rails laid 'cross the road. They could search for a better life, but no, they're way too dumb.

Pauline squeezed her face between Mama's shoulder and the car door. The thump, thump, thump, of the tires crossing the cattle guard made it final.

The sign of an end and a beginning...

* * * * *

Pauline spotted Daddy nervously glancing at the gas gauge.

"Daddy, are we about to run out of gas?"

"Tell ya the truth Pauline, if we pass one more boarded-up gas station we'd better be a prayin' this here car can run on fumes."

They hadn't passed anyone for miles when the car sputtered to a stop. The Sampley's sat motionless as if nothing the least bit unexpected had occurred. Pauline lost track of how long they sat there staring at the empty road ahead—must have been until the curious sound of a suffering car engine rolled up next to them. The Sampley's gawked at the carload of ragged folks peering through vacant eyes pasted on pale, smudged faces. The driver gazed at them, open-mouthed, from under an overflowing batch of possessions tied to the roof. "Need a tow?" He called out in a raspy voice.

"I'd be much obliged," Daddy replied hesitantly as if not certain the whole sight wasn't just a mirage.

The man spoke again, "Yep, I barely made it past those dried up service stations, myself. That's the way it is these days. Got a good strong rope in there someplace?"

The two men scooted under their car bumpers taking no notice of the bits of sand and gravel embedding themselves into the back of their sweat-soaked limbs. Bent knees and bulging veins revealed the strain of tying the stiff, heavy, rope under the frame of the car.

When the rope was as tight as a fiddle string, the Oakland began to roll. Pauline thought it a peculiar sight—the kids up ahead, heads bobbing back and forth, staring, and giggling. *It really takes the starch out of my pride, them a helpin' us out this way. Treatin' us like poor Okies, they are. Ugh, I wish we were doing the towing instead of them. Then she secretly rebuked herself—I can't believe I would let jealousy and wrongful pride take hold of me at a time like this. Shoot, if it wasn't for this rusty bucket of bolts a runnin' outta gas we would never have met these Good Samaritans who may very well be leadin' us out of the depths of Hell. Oops, good thing Mama didn't hear me say 'Hell' for God knows that no amount of trouble would keep her from huntin' down her bar of soap to 'wash the cussin' away." She gazed helplessly out the window—what in the world must we look like, the only life in the heart of nothingness?"*

Daddy removed his hat, hugged the steering wheel, and leaned in close to the windshield. Everyone's eyes were pinned on the tightly stretched tow-rope—*Our saving grace*, thought Pauline.

Emerging from a funnel of blowing sand, Pauline blinked to focus on the fuzzy outline of a building up ahead. Daddy periodically tapped the brakes, keeping the slack out of the rope as much as possible. Together, the two vehicles coasted to a stop in front of a faded red gas pump topped with a gauge. Daddy unfolded himself out of the driver's seat, "Whew! Alright Sampleys, everyone out."

The rowdy car at the other end of the rope peered at them like hoot owls stalking a mouse—then pushed and pulled their way over one another, escaping their confines. They ran toward the Sampley children who couldn't seem to decide whether to be beholding or bewildered. Dale captured their attention with his many questions.

"Where ya from?

Where ya goin'?

Whatcha gonna do when ya git there?"

Pauline, June, and Delbert each nodded a polite smile before going their separate ways—leaving the chumming to Dale.

Back behind the gas station, Pauline spied a clothesline stretched from the back stoop of a shabby, unpainted house to the side-door of the station. Dingy shirts, socks, and pants fought erratic wind gusts. Three stair-step kids used empty vegetable cans to dig in the sand next to a sagging screen door. *Well, least they have a home.*

Dale, still waving as their rescuers pulled away, amused himself by kicking rocks against the side of the service station wall knocking large chips of paint off with each blow.

Pauline sneakily walked up behind him.

"Dale, what do ya think you're doin'?"

"Whoa, ya scared me, Pauline! I was jest seein' if I could hit that poster up there on the wall."

The bright red of the new poster stood out against the drab, patchy green wall. "Well, Dale, find something else to entertain yourself. I want to see that poster and don't want to end up with a goose egg on the back of my head."

Dale stood alongside Pauline—flabbergasted; hands cupped over their mouths, they drew the attention of the rest of the family.

Daddy asked, "What does it say, June?"

Pancho's RODEO
3 NIGHTS
Highway 6 to Rosemond
Breakfast, Lunch, and Dinner
Bar Open

Without a word, all eyes fixed on the poster of a nude woman straddling the back of a long-horned steer—right arm cast high, fist clenched. A thick mane of strawberry blonde hair whirled purposely about her, a feeble attempt at modesty.

Mama gasped, her open palm pressed tight against her chest. "This has to be God's way of telling us we have done the right thing by leavin' Pancho's place."

* * * * *

On the road again, Daddy cleared his throat the way he always did when he was about to say something he didn't really want to say, "Delbert, ahem, Charles tells me he can git you work at the Golden Queen Mine in Mojave. You'd bunk down with him and his Uncle Amos for a while. The pay would be good for a boy your age."

Delbert leaned back hard against the rough upholstered car seat that had once been as soft as velvet. He listened intently while staring up at the shredded overhead cloth lining on the roof of the Oakland.

"Son, I know that if you had your druthers you would rather stay with the family, but fact is, you don't. Times may git a little worse before they git better. It's the way it has to be. The whole family is dependin' on us, you and I, to make ends meet."

Pauline imagined Delbert's mind was like a windmill on a blustery day. *I don't want to be dropped off in a strange town in the middle of the Mojave Desert! I'm afraid to go down into a dark, narrow mine shaft with a bunch of strange men. I'm not a man; I'm just a kid!* She stared at his watery eyes fixed on the road ahead, but his tears brought his misery out in the open for all to see.

Pauline turned her worry to Mama. Her face grimaced with pain—the flat of her hands firmly pushed against her stomach. Tight lips quivered above her dimpled chin. *I hope Mama's not going to cry,* thought Pauline. *I just won't be able to stand it if Mama cries.*

June, at the mere mention of Charles' name, oblivious to the emotions of the rest of the family, had escaped into her own world. She sat straight, shoulders back, eyes shifting from side to side across the landscape.

What is she so starry-eyed about? thought Pauline. *She only met him once. Guess he is the only thing she can think about.*

Only time I ever felt that way was with Runt. Wanted to be with him all the time. Wanted to talk to Runt 'bout everythin'. Maybe that is what love is? Maybe that is what June is lookin' for? How silly of me to even be thinkin' that way—Runt was just a dumb ol' pig."

Around mid-day, Daddy pulled alongside one of the water barrels, made available by the CCC boys, for filling radiators. Pauline had seen desperate folks drink from one of the barrels now and then, but Mama always said, "It's tainted." Huddled together on the shady side of the car, a meal of cold biscuits and beans was taken. Delbert broke the silence by asking, "Daddy, how much farther is Mojave?"

"Not far, son, not far—just down the road a piece."

Pauline asked, "How far is a piece, Daddy?"

"Oh not far, Pauline, not far."

Pauline crinkled her nose asking herself, *Did Daddy really answer my question or not?*

Delbert slung the bulging, canvas, water bag over the front bumper of the car. Without a word he climbed back into the backseat.

Ever since Daddy spoke of leaving Delbert off in Mojave, an

awkward hush filled the car. No singing. No quizzes. No license plate games. None of Mama's, silly, spur-of-the-moment games.

* * * * *

Daddy cranked the steering wheel hard, alternating, one hand over the other heading straight for the sign—Golden Queen Mine. He clung to the wheel as the Oakland wobbled down the washboard of a road, jostling the newcomers to and fro.

The word 'Office' was nearly worn off the door of a lean-to, first in a string of odd-shaped outbuildings. Daddy stepped out of the car shoving his shirttail down into his pants. He slid his hat down on his forehead with his thumb and forefinger the way he always did when he was jittery about something.

"Come on, Delbert, let's see what we can find out." As the two walked away side-by-side, it struck Pauline that Mama had not moved or spoken a word since Daddy first spoke of the Golden Queen Mine.

June, preoccupied with her search for Charles, ogled grimy-faced workers crammed into trucks, hard hats bobbing. With childlike innocence, she gave a group of miners gathered near the shaft entrance the once-over, too. Pauline gave June a bug-eyed stare —to no avail.

The ongoing trembling of the car, as Delbert rummaged through the contents stacked on top, grated on everyone's nerves. With his CCC bag of belongings tucked under one arm he walked around to Mama's window. Her eyes gazing on something only she could see, she muttered, "Good luck, son." For an instant, Delbert cocked his head to one side, cutting his eyes toward the sky as though puzzled by Mama's reaction. He turned and walked away shoulders slumped. He didn't look back.

June squealed when Charles appeared at her window just inches from her face, which was rapidly turning a striking shade of scarlet. Eyes fixed on June, Charles spoke to Mama, "Did Delbert get squared away okay, Mrs. Sampley?" Mama's silent stare brought about a look of concern that pulled him to her. He patted her forearm, "Don't worry, Ma'am, once you're settled in somewhere, I'll make sure Delbert spends plenty of time with you. Believe me, when a fella has a family like yours, he's one lucky guy."

Mama looked at Charles under heavy lids, her empty eyes glazed over with a pain too deep for tears. "I'd be much obliged, Charles," she said slipping back into the private world that seemed to be closing out everything and everyone around her.

Daddy slithered down into the driver's seat, "Yep, that Charles Jones, he's an alright guy. Golden Queen must be payin' him good. Drives a mighty fine car, he does. And the way he dressed when he came out to Pancho's, now that was somethin', fancy shoes and all." June's eyebrows arched with exaggerated aloofness. She straightened her shoulders and tilted her head up and away from Pauline. Daddy flashed a half grin at her by way of the rearview mirror, "Says he won't mind drivin' Delbert home once we get settled." June glanced nonchalantly out the window.

For the life of me I'll never understand her, thought Pauline. *First she is beside herself to see him, and a minute later, she doesn't care a lick. Sure beats me.*

The cavity Delbert's empty seat left behind filled the car with an emptiness that seemed to leave Mama mute. Daddy asked, "Fay, shall we pull over soon and grab us a bite to eat, maybe at the next water stop? Gotta keep that radiator full now, don't we?" Daddy placed his hand on Mama's knee rubbing it softly.

Pauline sighed edgily. *How can Daddy act like everything is normal when it's not.*

Unlike the Burma Shave signs that had filled the car with anticipation and laughter—passing the forlorn faces of squatter's camped along the roadside brought to mind only the fear of broken dreams. The squatters turned away at the sight of the Sampleys too; it's as if we're invisible, thought Pauline. She studied a twitching muscle in the back of Mama's neck. Mama was trembling and her breath unsteady.

As if Daddy were simply talking to himself and not expecting an answer he blurted out, "Here's where we're gonna park this here covered wagon for the night, Sampleys. Got any more of those biscuits and beans left, Fay?"

Oh no, thought Pauline. *My growling stomach is not calling for biscuits and beans again.* Suddenly the car swerved and bumped off the road.

June wrinkled her nose, asking fussily, "We are not going to sleep here are we?" Squealing brakes were her only reply. The Sampleys shuffled through their belongings digging out their bedrolls. Daddy began to whistle the tune to "Life is Just a Bowl of Cherries." Pauline couldn't help but sing along and then Dale harmonized with her.

Daddy passed the provisions for the night to the children, one at a time, until camp was set up. Up the road as far as the eye could see were silhouettes of others like them. Homeless.

Chapter Seventeen

*The morning sun awakened Pauline to the stench of her sweat-*soaked hair and dirt-caked fingernails. She flung the cover from her face. Rubbing the sleep from her eyes, she skimmed the wilderness for a clue to her whereabouts. *Ahhh, Daddy's bedroll pressed tight against Mamma's. His forearm, sunburned in the image of yesterday's shirtsleeve, lay over Mama's shoulder, fitting together like two spoons.*

Daddy propped himself up on one elbow. "I hear tell there's a government camp not too far from here. Those government camps are the best ya know; running water and ready-made canvas shelters. Not all the sickness ya find in the Hoovervilles. Yep, jobs ta be found. And even a school. Least we'll have a roof over our heads 'til we can see our way clear ta git us a place of our own, most likely in the city somewhar.

Somethin' musta snapped inside Mama's head at the thought of us Sampleys a livin' in a government camp after leavin' Delbert off at the mine an' all. Guess she jest couldn't take the thought of it after all the luxuries at Pancho's.

Mama lifted Daddy's arm off of her as if it were the branch of a sapling. Mournfully, she began rolling up her bed, tying it with a piece of twine. She teetered toward the car cradling her bedroll like a newborn babe. Pauline's heart raced at the sight. The puffing of her own shallow breath echoed in her ears. *What has happened to Mama? And Daddy, he carries on like it's just another day?*

Interrupting Pauline's conversation, Daddy called out, "June, get out Mama's lye soap. We ain't gonna go pullin' in there lookin' like a bunch of Okies. We'll wash up, then be on our way. The immigrant camp ain't more than a few hours away."

I hate those words, immigrant camp, thought Pauline.

* * * * *

Off in the distance, Pauline spotted hundreds of colorless tents, surrounded by miles of nothingness. *Well, I'll be. If that ain't a sight.*

Daddy swung the car down a long, narrow road leading past rows of boxy, canvas-clad, homesteads. "We'll drive on through — take a gander first." Daddy cleared his throat and fiddled with the brim of his hat.

Mama rested her head on the back of the car seat and crossed her hands over her stomach; closing her eyes tight. Even though Daddy seemed to be driving at a snail's pace, a cloud of dust rose up behind them. Some folks gave them a nod or a wave, while others seemed to look right through them.

Pauline leaned forward, resting her chin on Daddy's shoulder. "Look, Daddy, there's the office."

Daddy swung the Oakland around to the door, tires spewing a

backlash of fine sand. June coughed dramatically while appearing to fan the dust out the window. Daddy seemed not to notice, stepping off of the running board of the car with apparent, newfound confidence.

"You all wait here. Dale and I are gonna see if we can find out what this here camp is all about." Dale walked tall as he kept in stride with Daddy.

Sticking his head back out the office door Daddy gave a sharp whistle. Pauline hollered out the window, "Whatcha want, Daddy?"

"Send your Mama over here. I need some readin' and writin' done." Everyone waited breathlessly. Mama didn't rush to Daddy's side. The truth lay before them, loud and clear—Mama was mindless to Daddy's plea for help. *Funny, the things I never noticed before,* thought Pauline. *Mama was always there for all of us. Daddy always called her his right-hand man, and now... Well, I don't know who my Mama is anymore.*

June sprang into action as if Daddy had called for her. For a split second, she fondly gazed at Mama then stroked her frail shoulder.

June yelled from the car window, "I'll help you, Daddy."

Daddy leaned in close to June. "Got to fill out these here papers. They say there's work at some DiGiorgio's farm—sortin' an' pickin' grapes. S'pose ta be close by. They say I should be able to start on Monday mornin'."

When the three emerged from the registration shack, Pauline scanned their faces for a sign of their future. She observed Daddy holding June's hand as they chatted back and forth smiling and talking excitedly. Giving June a hand onto the running board of the Oakland Daddy announced, "All set? Let's pull 'er on down to site number 189."

Mama stayed in the car while the rest of the family stood in the middle of their new home surrounded by roll-up canvas walls and a canvas ceiling overhead. Daddy and the children passed the items from the car hand over hand to Pauline and June who attempted to place their belongings without Mama's guidance.

Daddy smiled in a way Pauline had not seen for a long time, his eyes glistened as he spoke, "You girls kin surprise Mama by fixin' things up—you know—make it look homey."

Pauline peeked out to check on Mama in the car. *Is she asleep or staring off into space with her eyes half open?*

Pauline wondered how in the world June knew where to start? There she was arranging boxes, unpacking clothes and pots and pans; all the while acting like its play instead of work. *Or is she tryin' to show off by stepping into Mama's shoes?*

For once Pauline was grateful when June told her what to do, "Go find a waterspout somewhere and wash the dirt off anything we eat off of."

Pauline loaded the black cast iron skillet, a small dented aluminum pan with a missing handle, and a paring and butcher knife into Mama's soap kettle. Searching, she found three flour sacks that Mama must have tucked away to make dish towels, dresses or aprons. She loaded one of the sacks with their eating utensils, metal pie and dinner plates, a large wooden spoon, and fruit and jelly jars into two of the bags doubled together for strength.

Twisting the top of the sack together tightly, she shaped two dog-ear handles out of the rough cotton fabric. Resting the bag on top of one foot, she scooted it across the floor inch by inch remembering how she had once danced with Daddy by standing on his feet as he glided across the floor.

June chided, "PAULINE, what in the world is the wisdom in stuffing everything in one bag? Don't be so lazy, just come back for a second load." Ignoring her comment, Pauline pressed on while trying to calm her grunts and groans. Standing outside the tent, she wiped the sweat from her brow with her forearm to the tune of June's unending criticism.

"Pauline, you are impossible! Daddy trusts us to take care of things, and you are doing nothing but wasting time!"

Pauline hollered back, "Don't try to be such a know-it-all, June. Can't cha remember nothin'? Don't cha remember Mama a sayin', waste not—want not? I'm tryin' to save time by cuttin' down on trips. Don't cha think Mama knew what she was a talkin' bout, huh? And you know as well as I do that I'd rather take a beatin' than disappoint Daddy."

A few startled women, some old and frail, others young with bellies swollen tight with child, threw open their tent flaps at the sound of the clinking and scraping of Pauline's wares. She slung her bag behind her allowing it to drag on the ground when the weight became too heavy. She attempted to lengthen her steps with her head held high,

Safely past the gawkers, Pauline thought, *Don't know why I can't ever listen to June, after all, she is my big sister. But, no. I'm such a dadburn know-it-all, and now I'm lost in this here strange place toting something bigger than I am. . . and it's gettin' heavier by the minute. And what is the only thing I can think of—June must never know that I bit off more than I could chew. What a sorry soul I am.*

As if she were walking on a washboard, Pauline hobbled on oversized shoes that were rapidly rubbing blisters on her heels. She spoke to herself. *I am in a real pickle this time, but I'm sure as sin not goin' to ask one of them busybodies for help and make myself look like some pea-brained Okie or somethin'.*

Let's see now, where in the heck would that water spout be? Well, there's an outhouse, must be a tap 'round here somewhars.

She thought out loud, *Guess we may be okay here for a while if Mama gets back to herself again.*

Darn if I didn't pass that blasted waterspout. Girl, keep your head about you. That's what Mama would say if she were here, yep, that's what she'd say all right.

On the way back Pauline wandered in and out of the maze of tents. Sorry eyes of other residents met Pauline's, but she quickly looked the other way swallowing her sobs. She stopped to shake the numbness from her fingers. She stared down at the sight of hot, fluid-filled, blisters rising up on the palms of her hands. Answered prayer! She spotted the front end of the Oakland, poking out from beside their temporary homestead, empty water bag in place.

Red-faced, Pauline straightened her shoulders before pushing the canvas flap to their tent back with one elbow and sidestepping through the entrance. Loud enough for all to hear, she boasted, "Well, that's a job well done." Biceps still trembling, she lifted the bag off of her shoulder, trying not to gasp with pain—imagining her skin rubbed raw.

Not looking up from her task at hand, June instructed, "Unload everything into those crates stacked in the corner. Put the things we won't use every day on the bottom. Stack them neatly now."

Without words, Pauline mouthed June's orders behind her back, while noticing Daddy attempting to stifle a smile.

"Come on," Daddy said to Dale. "Let's take a walk—get our bearings outside before dark sets in. Give the girls room to work."

Pauline abruptly turned toward Daddy, eyes green with envy.

* * * * *

Drenched with sweat, Pauline and June perched themselves on two wooden chairs in the middle of the room next to the rough semblance of a table. While pridefully searching their surroundings, they marveled at their work.

Daddy's arm stretched through the parted canvas front door allowing Dale to walk in first. "Hey, look at this here place, mighty spiffy, don't ya think, son?" Daddy sturdily patted Dale's shoulder seeming to jar a comment out of him.

"Oh, yeah, uh, looks good," he said cutting his eyes around, taking in the perfect placing of the laundry tub, pots and pans, their clothes, bedrolls, crates, and chairs.

Pauline leaped to her feet, "Daddy, can I wake Mama to show her what we've done?"

Daddy pressed his forefinger lightly against sealed lips, "That's my job, Pauline," he said with a wink.

* * * * *

Mama clutched Daddy's arm while taking slow, deliberate steps across the room. Taking both of her hands, he lowered her trembling body as if she were a china doll, onto a chair. A look of fatigue slid over Mama's colorless face.

Daddy pushed Mama's hair away from her eyes, "There honey, you rest a spell now; you're jest worn to a frazzle. Sleep is all ya need to get back to yer old self again. The kids and I will fix us up a nice warm supper."

What on earth will we come up with that will even come close to a nice warm supper? thought Pauline. *There is not enough here to feed one, much less four.* She detested the fact that her eyebrows gave away her doubt as they uncontrollably slithered up her forehead.

Daddy was searching through what was left of their meager supplies when they heard the sound of a woman's voice, "Hello, Hello."

Before they could reply a sweet, round-faced lady pushed their stiff canvas door open with her plentiful backside. "I'm Mrs. Jackson, the schoolteacher." She appeared clutching the handle of a steaming cast iron kettle. The Sampleys stared in awe until Daddy said, "Here, Mrs. Jackson, let me take that off your hands."

Pauline fixed her gaze on Mrs. Jackson as she dished up five bowls of cabbage soup speckled with tiny pieces of carrots. Mrs. Jackson's voice sounded as soft as butter and somehow familiar, like family. "I would like to invite your children to attend classes tomorrow," her eyes shifted from Dale to Pauline and June. She glanced at Daddy. "I'll stop by in the morning to walk with them if you like." Pauline wanted to scream, *Who will care for Mama while we are at school?*

Daddy changed the subject, "Don't know how we'll ever thank ya. By the way, I'm Jack Sampley, and this here is my wife, Fay. Mama's fixed stare moved slowly toward the woman's face. She did not speak. Mrs. Jackson sat on an overturned crate next to Mama holding a small bowl of the warm soup. She seemed oblivious to Mama's unfocused greyish eyes.

Daddy quickly replied, "Fay has been in dire need of rest. I'm afraid the trip took quite a toll on her. She'll be fit as a fiddle in no time, though. These here are our youngin's, June, Pauline, and Dale. Our oldest son, Delbert is workin' at the Golden Queen Mine. He should be here for a visit before long."

Mrs. Jackson's smile bared a bountiful set of the whitest teeth Pauline had ever seen. The creases that formed at the outside corners of her eyes seemed to tug at a bun perched squarely on top of her head. "Well," she said, "I don't want to keep you, Mr. Sampley." She then bent at the waist until she was eye level with Pauline, Dale, and June, "So, we'll see you three at school tomorrow?"

While Daddy walked Mrs. Jackson to the lane, Pauline eavesdropped enough to hear Mrs. Jackson speaking in a near whisper, "Don't worry about your wife, Mr. Sampley, it happens a lot around here. A woman just wears down and needs a little time. Holding the family up through thick and thin can be a heavy burden to bear. Let her have her time; she'll come out of it. I have a hunch that your girls are smart enough to practice some of what, I suspect, their Mama taught them over the years. This may just be their time to shine."

"Well, we sure are much obliged, Mrs. Jackson, for everything."

"Love thy neighbor as thy self, right, Mr. Sampley?"

Pauline noticed Mama take a few small sips of her soup and then push the bowl away. Stillness overcame everyone as she shuffled to her bedroll and stretched out on her side, facing the wall, arm kinked over her face.

Daddy raised his harmonica to his lips and began to play "Down in the Valley" followed by "Barbry Allen." Pauline thought, *It's Daddy's gift from God—I know it is. Daddy always knows when we are about to feel downtrodden, and he knows how to ease our jitters. How I love him for that. Even under swollen lids, his gentle eyes can't be hidden. He must surely be like the Heavenly Father that Mama knows.*

At the sound of "Barbry Allen," Mama turned to listen. A fleeting smile crossed her face.

Just before sunset, Daddy said, "Let's walk around the camp, kids—git a feel for the place. Let your Ma rest. We'll fill her in on everything in the mornin'."

As the foursome strolled, Pauline relished the sound of children playing hide and seek, stickball, and kick the can. She inhaled deeply, drawing in the strong scent of a campfire burning somewhere.

Daddy and the children were drawn to the strum of a pair of guitars, and a cluster of shadows huddled together. Pauline strained to soak up all the sounds and scents of the night. One of the guitar players chatted with the group that was quickly gathering. In a raspy voice, he mumbled that their next song was taken from an old English folk song—it's original title was called "The Unfortunate Rake".

> *As I walked out in the streets of Laredo,*
> *As I walked out in Laredo one day*
> *I spied a poor cowboy wrapped up in white linen,*
> *Wrapped up in white linen as cold as the clay.*

Daddy slipped his harmonica out of his pocket, sat down on a crate, and played along.

Chapter Eighteen

Like a thunderbolt, June appeared in front of Pauline's face. She whispered loudly, "Daddy left for work before sun up. He said Dale will go to school with Mrs. Jackson and you and I are to stay here with Mama. He put me in charge."

Sitting up in bed, hair going every which way, Dale whined, "Doggone it, why do I have to be the one to go to school?"

"Because Daddy said so," said Pauline quickly glancing at Mama to be sure she wasn't disturbed by her motherly comment.

June glared past them muttering through clinched teeth, "We're not supposed to upset Mama. Now, I'll see what I can scrounge up for breakfast," she whispered. "Then we'll get you off to school and make sure that Mama eats, just like Daddy said."

June's eyes darted from the cooking supplies stacked in the corner to Dale, who was still in the fetal position on his bed, and to Mama, on her back now hands folded over her waist, eyes closed.

Pauline recognized the telltale signs of June on a mission—*so like Mama.*

June pursed her lips close to Dale's ear, "Now take that bar of lye soap and get yourself down to the water faucet. Pauline you and I will sit with Mama—try to get her to eat something.

"Take this pitcher and bring me back some water. While you are gone, I'll get the stove started so that we can give Mama a hot breakfast, and heat some water so we can wash her.

"Then I'll carry the washboard and our dirty clothes down to the laundry house. You'll stay here with Mama. See if you can get her out for some fresh air. It'll do her good. You wash up too. You know how Mama likes that."

"Think I'll put Mama's Treasure Chest out where she can see it when she opens her eyes."

"Okay, Pauline, and if you run out of things to do, you can get down on your knees and pray that that nice Mrs. Jackson will keep her word and visit Mama once in a while. It'd be good for her to have a friend."

With each passing day, Mama seemed to get thinner and thinner. Pauline hated herself for her impatience. It seemed everyone was out of sorts and feeling helpless in the face of Mama's depression.

The silence was loudest after supper. June only served to irritate Pauline by trying to fill in for Mama's Bible reading. She whispered under her breath, *Shut up June, I don't wanna hear you!* June seemed unmindful at the annoyance her awkward attempt brought forth.

Once in a while, June would slap the Bible down on Pauline's lap saying, "Here, you read this time!" Pauline always thrust it right back at her, lips tight, shaking her head from side to side. Helpless guilt washed over Pauline as she noticed her actions made Mama's eyelids flutter and her brows scrunch tight together.

One night when June laid the Bible across Pauline's lap, she didn't pass it back. It was open to Psalm 23. Mama had read the verses aloud over and over. She had retold the story in her own words many times. Pauline had it memorized. She sat fingering the worn and tattered page thoughtfully.

"Ahem."

Mama blinked rapidly. Daddy slowly rustled a thin square of tobacco paper between his thumb and forefinger.

Pauline's words spilled forth. "*The Lord is my shepherd;*" she stopped to look at Mama, "He thinks of us as his precious sheep."

"*I shall not want.* He gives us everything we need and He will take care of us through the tough times.

"*He maketh me to lie down in green pastures;* Mama, you always told us that He watches over us like a shepherd watches over his sheep—He WANTS us to rest.

"*He restoreth my soul; He leadeth me in the paths of righteousness for his name's sake. Yea, though I walk through the valley of the shadow of death, I will fear no evil; thy rod and thy staff they comfort me.*

"Remember what you always told us, Mama, He protects us—keeps us safe.

"Leaving our place on the Ranch was hard, but it was right, wasn't it Mama? It sure as heck seemed like a dark valley we was a goin' through... Fact is, though, Daddy has a job. We have a roof over our head. Charles will be bringin' Delbert to us soon, and June and I will be startin' Mrs. Jackson's school tomorrow—so as we kin get real smart like you, Mama!"

Pauline kneeled down in front of Mama. Tears spilled from

under her strawberry blonde lashes. "Can you hear me, Mama? Can you?"

Slowly, Pauline's hand came to rest upon Mamas. Together the tender young hand directed the hand that in the past had changed her diapers, sewn her dresses, cooked her meals, and wiped her tears away. It all came flooding back as the fingers of the young and the old intertwined, coming to rest on the ragged pages. Pauline read aloud in her best English with more confidence than ever before.

"Thou preparest a table before me in the presence of mine enemies; thou anointest my head with oil; my cup runneth over. Surely goodness and mercy shall follow me all the days of my life, and I will dwell in the house of the LORD forever.

"Mama, you always said, no house will ever be as beautiful as our Heavenly Home. And when Daddy tucked us in on our last night in the Texas Panhandle, his words were, 'We may be poor, but we will always be together.' Well, Mama, we have been together, but you haven't been with us! And, oh, how we have missed you."

Mama folded the wrong side of the large collar on her dress up over her eyes to wipe the tears gushing forth, as if dammed up for months. Her arms stretched wide as she motioned for her brood to come to her. Fingers dovetailed together around Mama's waist and cleansed by their individual sobs of relief—the Sampleys were whole again.

That night the family lay on their bedrolls, head to head, talking long into the night. Stories of times past—of bootlegging, crop picking, fond memories of Runt, and gathering eggs while fighting off that cantankerous rooster.

In the morning Mama was up and dressed before anyone else. Pauline lay awake watching by the dim light of a kerosene lamp, as she moved quietly back and forth across the floor humming ever so softly,

> *On a hill far away stood an old rugged cross,*
> *The emblem of suff'ring and shame;*
> *And I love that old cross where the Dearest and Best*
> *For a world of lost sinners was slain.*

Pauline prayed, a silent prayer, *Thank you, Lord. What a blessing to hear Mama's voice once again.*

* * * * *

Mama slid her arms around Daddy's neck and pressed her cheek close to his. Her lips pressed wide into a soft smile forcing her cheeks to spread even wider apart. "You know Jack; I believe I recall Mrs. Jackson telling me that there is a dairy nearby where we can get milk free! She said the farmer usually throws out the skimmed milk. You have to take your own jars though. He used to sell it for five cents per gallon before the health department stopped him. Think I'll walk over yonder and get us some today."

She ruffled the top of his hair as he grabbed both of her arms to pull her close.

* * * * *

"How was school today, kids?" Everyone excitedly began to answer at once. "Wait, wait, wait," Mama said with a content glow. "One at a time, please!" Mama seemed to be drinking in every word as she waited for each to tell of their day's activities.

Pauline spoke first, "We start each morning with a salute to the flag, a hymn, and a prayer and sing a song called, 'I Love You California.' Felt like a traitor. Made me miss Texas."

"Why, I never heard of such a thing? How does it go?"

Pauline cleared her throat, and with a silly grin she screeched out the words:

I love you California . . . you're the greatest state of all.

I love you in the winter, summer, spring, and fall.

I love your fertile valleys, your dear mountains I adore.

I love your grand old ocean, and I love her rugged shore.

Mama interrupted, "Well, I'll be—I had no idea."

After school the next day, Pauline noticed a commotion in front of one of the neighbors' tents. She picked bits and pieces out of the grim conversations drifting from several small groups that had gathered.

"...coughing, feverish baby, fighting for his breath. No one knows what to do. Could be pneumonia." Pauline ran toward Mama who was sitting out front of their homestead. She talked so fast that all Mama could make out was that there was a sick baby in camp and it was serious.

Just as Pauline suspected, Mama sprang into action, "Get me a pair of socks, Pauline. June, you get the salt. Dale, you start the wood stove—we'll need to heat some salt bags."

Mama scurried up the lane to a tent where a tall, gaunt, looking man paced outside. Ignoring him, she rushed past, toward the raspy, choking sounds of the baby's cry. "Oh, the poor thing needs to loosen the mucus in his chest."

A somber group gathered around the father of the baby just outside their tent. They cleared a way for the three Sampley children as they rushed to Mama's side with the requested supplies.

Mama motioned for their quick departure nearly as soon as they arrived. Seemed like forever before the crying stopped and Mama stepped out, red-faced, perspiration-soaked hair clinging to her forehead and neck. Soggy salt bags dangled from both hands as she shook her head slowly. "Too far gone, too far gone," she whispered.

Candles burned dimly beside the tiny casket, a wood box with the words, *California Oranges* stamped on one side. Pauline keenly studied the way the grown-ups lingered around the remaining family.

Some mornings on the way to school, Pauline noticed ladies in faded flour sack dresses carrying the grieving family's laundry out of their tent. Other times the women placed steaming hot kettles of food just outside their door so as not to disturb their mourning.

Pauline wondered if the nighttime cries of a mother would ever end, or if it would be possible to forget the sound. After a while, it became common to see different families escorting the parents of the dead child to weekly dances and talent shows held around the campfire. Pauline soaked it all in—filing it away for who knows when.

* * * * *

Since all camp events were open to the public, Charles was often invited to spend the weekend. Daddy was adamant, though, about Charles, an unmarried man sleeping under the same roof as his girls. He didn't mind making it clear, either, that June would not be going anywhere with Charles in his car. However, Charles was allowed to take meals and attend dances or gatherings with the family. Charles seemed pleased just to be with June, any time, any place. Pauline wondered why.

* * * * *

June and Pauline lay side by side, snuggled down into their bedrolls, arms folded behind their heads. Together they stared up at the soft billowing of the tent roof.

"Wasn't tonight fun, June?"

"It sure was, Pauline. You know what? You are a real good dancer. You kept perfect time to that fiddle tonight. You have a lot of rhythm."

"Why thanks, June, I didn't see you and Charles dancin' much. You were mostly gazin' into his eyes 'round the campfire."

Pauline hesitated, then swallowed hard, "June, do you love Charles?"

"Ummm, well, Pauline, guess I haven't thought about it in quite that way, but yes, I suppose I do. I do love Charles."

"How do you know, June?"

"Now, Pauline, just what have you noticed that's different about me since I met Charles?"

"Ummmm, let me think. For one thing, when Charles is around, you don't seem to hear or listen to anyone but him. Ugh, it's really frustrating at times. And, for that matter, when he is away, your mind is always wandering, and you seem so dreamy all the time," said Pauline while rolling her eyes and waving both hands, gracefully, through the air.

June punched Pauline causing her to fake pain and suppress a giggle.

"It's just impossible for you to understand, Pauline. It's just indescribable."

Whispering, so as not to wake the rest of the family, Pauline asked, "June, don't you think it is your duty, as the older sister, to prepare me for such things as loooveee?"

June crossed her arms stiffly over her chest and pressed her lips together, chin up. "If you are going to be silly about it, we're done talking,"

"Okay, I'll be serious. Just tell me how I'll know. I have to be prepared for what's to come."

"Ahem. First of all, you will find that you will not be able to focus on much of anything, but him. You will feel like smiling nearly all the time. Remember when Runt was born? You couldn't take your eyes off of him, right? Didn't you want to hold him and take care of him all the time? I even saw you kiss Runt on the snout, once or twice, right?

June cut her eyes toward Pauline teasingly, with a smirk.

Pauline sucked in a big breath and held it, hand tightly cupped over her mouth. "So, that's what it is like? June, are you saying Charles has kissed you?"

"Well, maybe."

"Holy cow. You're not serious. Are you?"

"Pauline, calm down, or you'll wake Mama and Daddy and then you won't be able to learn a thing. Now, some things to know are: He may pretend to yawn and then slip his arm around your shoulder. Then he will gradually slide closer and closer to you by pretending to get more comfortable. When this happens, you just pretend not to notice and that all is normal. If you should feel his breath on your cheek, you are about to be kissed, and that is about the last straw. His slightly parted lips will feel like warm milk. At that point, believe me, you will have to push yourself away. So, that's the story of love... as I know it."

Pauline held her quilt tightly over her face muffling the mixture of giggles and snorts. June couldn't help but join in until the two lay with their hands across their stomachs to calm the pain of their suppressed laughter. Eventually, after the peaceful quiet that followed, Pauline whispered, "Thanks, June."

* * * * *

Mrs. Jackson soon realized that Mama was born to be a schoolteacher and recruited her as her assistant. The class was so crowded that many students sat on the floor—book and pencil balanced on their lap. Pauline often found herself glancing around the room to spot Mama leaning over a student's desk, reading to a small group, or down on her haunches using buttons for arithmetic counters on the worn, wooden floor.

Pauline often felt an odd mixture of pride and selfishness whenever one of her fellow students ran toward Mama during recess. Seeing them throw their arms around her waist, and press themselves to her, caused Pauline to feel sinful pangs of jealousy.

Over the years, much to the chagrin of the rest of the Sampleys, Mama had insisted on hauling her treadle sewing machine across the country with her. Eventually, it became a comforting sight to see the piece sitting in the corner of the room—sackcloth, scissors, thread, and needles on top.

Regularly after school, several neighbor girls gathered at the Sampleys' for sewing lessons. Each waited patiently for their turn to sew their piece of cloth into something wearable. They learned to slide the coarse feed sack fabric under the pressure foot; to turn the wheel operating the needle until the material was pierced. Their bare feet pumped the large, ornate iron foot pedal pulling the belt around and around to the hum of the needle moving through the cloth. Mama always said, "All girls should learn to sew."

* * * * *

As the Sampley's slept, a rustle outside the tent awoke Daddy. He quietly walked to the door. Pulling the flap aside, he jumped back at the sight of Charles and Delbert. "Ummm, ummm, Mama is going to be beside herself. She has no idea. Delbert go wake her."

"Delbert, honey, you are here so soon. I don't believe it. I never... where is Charles? Let me fix you something to eat. You must be starved."

Now that everyone was awake, the group huddled around the orange crate table that Daddy had put together. It sat off kilter on the warped pine floor. In the dim kerosene light they chatted and ate until Daddy reminded everyone that, "Tomorrow is a work day."

Daddy and Charles stepped outside to roll one last cigarette before Charles bedded down in his car. In the quiet of the night the two inhaled while leaning back against the Oakland. Daddy searched the starlit sky while taking another drag off his cigarette. "Mighty purty, Charles, ain't she?"

"Yes, Mr. Sampley, she sure is. And speaking of pretty, I would like to talk to you about your daughter, June. You surely must know how much I admire and respect her. Mr. Sampley, I have such a strong desire to love her, care for her, and protect her... for the rest of her life."

Daddy flicked his cigarette to the ground, slowly twisting it into the dirt with the toe of his boot. He pushed his hat farther back on his head. He turned to stand directly in front of Charles. "Yep, guess I know'd it was a comin' and ta be honest, had it been anybody else, I'd have had them a hightailin' it outta here long ago."

Daddy reached out to shake Charles' hand. "Charles, I want cha to call me 'Jack' from now on. And she has to graduate from high school before you two take off for Las Vegas to get married. The family will go with you, of course. Got to give her away properly. Already feel like yer one of us."

"Jack, I never knew there were families like this. My parents divorced when the Depression hit. My mother took off for California, and I never knew where my dad ended up. But he made arrangements for me to live with my Aunt Sally. She was a kind woman, and put me through two years of college. But now, I realize, I never really had a true family."

* * * * *

The Sampley family and Charles walked slowly toward the waves of orange, purple, and pink that seemed to introduce the sunrise. Daddy cleared his throat, the way he did when he was about to say something important.

"All of the extra we earn, working as a family on the weekends, will go in the tobacco can. That is the money we will use to get jobs in the city and buy a home of our own. Yep, just like when we crossed that ol' Cally border, we Sampleys work for a better life. And when our big chance comes, we'll have the greenbacks set aside to skedaddle outta here." Each one nodded an understanding smile.

In the distance, they could see the contours of a few of the others who must have gathered earlier. Once at the assigned spot, Pauline wandered off to join her new sewing group. Mama immediately talked school with Mrs. Jackson. Daddy became engrossed in a conversation of farming and better days. Of course, June and Charles stood off to themselves, arm-in-arm, talking quietly. Pauline caught sight of June drawing circles in the dirt with one toe while cutting her flirty eyes in Charles' direction a time or two.

The wood slated sides on the DiGiorgio truck rattled and shook as it made a quick U-turn. Those already onboard leaned to one side and then reared back toward the cab as the truck reluctantly skidded to a stop. Daddy linked his hands together to give Mama a boast onto the splintered bed that leaned in the direction of a low tire.

Pauline noticed Charles placing his hands lightly around June's waist and lifting her on board as delicately as a freshly laid egg. As the truck pulled away, Pauline joined the younger children who attempted to balance straddle-legged, arms outstretched, in the middle of the truck-bed until the adults told them to "Sit."

*****

At the end of the day, walking home from the truck stop, Charles and June lagged behind the others. Charles reached for June's hand, pulling her to a stop. Then reaching for her other hand, he gazed into her eyes. "June, I asked your Daddy for your hand in marriage. I told him that I wanted to be with you for the rest of our lives. I love you, June."

"You asked Daddy's permission to marry me? Why, Charles,

you're such a gentleman. I have never heard of anyone around here doing anything like that. You want to marry me? What a lucky girl I am. The man I love wants to marry me. Of course, I can't wait."

"We'll have to wait, June, at least a few more weeks until you graduate from high school."

"Just think, Charles, in a matter of weeks we'll be married. It's a dream come true. I do love you so, Charles."

"Your Daddy says that we should have enough saved for he and Delbert to take off job and house hunting soon after your graduation. So, before they leave, your Mama and Daddy will stand up with us before the Justice of the Peace in Las Vegas."

Picking up the pace to catch up with the rest of the family, June shouted while spinning herself around and around. "Guess what? Charles and I are going to become husband and wife."

Pauline couldn't help beaming with delight as Daddy handed her the family's earnings. She wondered if it could be a trick to spur her on to take more of an interest in arithmetic. But, even an underlying motive could not dampen her pride in this important task.

Pauline carefully added the amounts she had written on her tablet over the past few weeks. "Ya think we'll be able to save enough, Pauline," Daddy said with half a grin. "These weekend jobs we git at 40 cents an hour, with all of us a workin', will add up fast. Plus, Mama gets 15 cents an hour for helpin' out Mrs. Jackson at the schoolhouse, jest more gravy."

"Too bad us kids don't get paid for our camp jobs," whined Pauline jokingly. She held her pencil high over her tally sheet. "Now, let's see, even if we got us 10 cents for each of the two outhouses we clean every Saturday morning, plus 10 cents for picking up the trash and garbage on our lane, and then 10 cents for mopping the washhouse floor and walls, well right there, we'd get 40 cents a week more."

Pauline was mortified by the look of disappointment on Daddy's face followed by the dreaded,

"Ahem. Heaven only knows where we would be without these camp folks a givin' us a chance to better ourselves. Everyone has to pitch in, so as we all have a good safe place to stay until we can venture out on our own again. Pauline, what has Mama's Bible readin' taught ya 'bout times such as these?"

Pauline's voice trembled with embarrassment at her noticeable lack of gratitude for their camp home. *"We are rooted and built up in Him, and established in the faith, as ye have been taught, abounding therein with thanksgiving.* Colossians 2:7."

"Well, if you ain't somethin', um, um, such a quick learner. Makes your Daddy mighty proud, Runt."

Pauline smiled with downcast eyes, "You know, Daddy, when I think about it—gettin' hired on to pick up trash for our lane has been a true blessin'. June and I found a pair of red high heel shoes that she wore to the dance that next Saturday night. We got Delbert a broken pocket-watch to fix and sell. For Mama, we spotted a pretty good piece of cloth for makin' her quilts, only needed a good scrubbin'. And for June, two books with just a few pages missing.

"It puts me to mind of Philippians 4:19. *My God shall supply all your needs.* And another thing, Daddy... we get to practice humility. Yep, pulling that garbage wagon along that bumpy lane, mercy me, there ain't nobody gettin' any sleep 'round here. Gets us a lot o' stares, that's for sure."

Pauline chuckled, "Course, Dale makes things worse when he hitches a ride on the back of the wagon, pinching his nose against the stink." Daddy threw his head back emitting a hoarse laugh.

Pauline continued, "Daddy, one day, June dared me to pick a maggot out of the garbage pail. When I plucked it out, and she saw it creeping up my hand, she threw up." Both curled over with laughter until they stood puffing, holding their ribs trying to catch their breath.

Pauline rested her head against Daddy's shoulder, "Yes, I am glad I have learned humility, it must be important, as many times as Mama has read us 1 Peter 5:5. Don't ya think, Daddy?"

Chapter Nineteen

Mama had a habit of shooing flies off the splintery crate-table in the midst of their tent. Over time, Pauline had developed a fondness for that old tabletop. This had become the heart of their home where meals were taken, decisions were made, and homework was done.

She loved the way one side of their tent could be rolled up to reveal the shade of Mama's castor bean plant. It warmed her heart to watch Mama water it daily with leftover dishwater. Pauline thought it a luxury to see something green and to hear the sound of the leaves rustle and quiver at any hint of a breeze.

* * * * *

Mama scrunched her nose causing deep wrinkles to appear on her forehead—she grunted at the sight of a fly slowly crawling toward Pauline's plate. She slid herself closer to Pauline while shooing at the critter, as Pauline finished her breakfast.

"Pauline, flies carry horrible diseases, and Lord knows we don't need more sickness around here. And what's worse is those camp officials and their pesticides. If that spray kills mosquitos, just imagine what it does to us."

Once, Mama got word that the County Health Department was sending nurses to inoculate camp families. She marched the whole family down to the camp office in a hurry.

Some neighboring families were looked down upon because they felt the vaccines were the Devil's work. They refused to let their children receive the vaccinations, thinking the government or the state was trying to kill them—to get rid of the filthy Okies, as some called them.

* * * * *

Most evenings were spent gathered around the community campfire. It seemed to be the only way to keep track of what was going on in the world. The younger children would start up games of tag or stickball while their elders spoke of impending war in Europe.

"Heard tell today that the Germans have invaded Poland."

"Yep, America will be gettin' involved; you can bet on it. Only right, I guess."

"Course us a gettin' involved in a war is gonna mean shippin' supplies to England. We gotta support 'em. After all, we are Americans."

"What do you think that will mean fer jobs right here in Californie?"

"Well, fellas, I think jobs are gonna skyrocket. Bet the pay will be mighty temptin' for those jobs, too."

"Sure would be nice to set some money aside and get the family set up in a place of our own before enlisting."

"Enlisting? I hear tell that we may be in for the first peacetime draft in United States history."

Pauline had only been half listening while pushing red coals around the fire pit with a twisted piece of rusty barbed wire. She perked up at the thought of jobs, though didn't interrupt. She wondered if the war would be a blessing or a curse?

* * * * *

Pauline, June, and Mama had prowled the fabric store for nearly an hour before June made her decision—a plain red skirt with a red and white polka dot blouse, and a red satin ribbon bow at the collar.

Early in the morning on graduation day, Pauline took the red high heels to the washhouse. She scrubbed the shoes well and buffed them dry.

"Mama may I git—"

"It is 'get,' Pauline,"

"—the Lavaliere out of your Treasure Chest, now?"

"All right, Pauline, why don't you clean and polish it while you're at it? It surely must be tarnished from sitting so long. I'll make you up a paste of baking soda and water. Get a sock from that box over there. You can use that for a polish rag.

'Walk with me to Mrs. McCormick's. She offered up her kitchen for baking June's graduation cake. You know... she's Daddy's boss' wife? Guess she appreciated the way I taught her little

Hank to read."

Pauline had already tuned out everything around her, "Think I'll carry the Lavaliere right here in the Treasure Chest, so as not to drop it in the dirt or somethin'."

"'Something,' not 'somethin'.'"

"Ugh, okay, Mama."

Pauline sat on a stool with her forearms propped on the bright red countertop. She slipped the worn-out sock over her hand and dipped it slightly into the paste Mama had made. Laying the Lavaliere on a dish towel, she leaned over close, pushing hard with tiny circles into the small intricate cutouts in the thin metal surrounding a petite ruby and dangling rough-cut pearl. Straining to keep her eyes from crossing, she buffed the necklace to a soft shine.

"Mama, tell me about the graduation and the wedding again."

"Oh Pauline, I just told you word by word yesterday!"

Pauline could tell that Mama wasn't really annoyed by her request at all, because she proceeded to explain in great detail.

"Well Pauline, first of all, as you may recall, there will only be four high school graduates this year. So of course, we are all very proud of your sister."

Pauline's jaw tightened as she wondered if Mama's words were slyly directed toward her.

Mama continued, "The four students will be inside the schoolhouse until the school bell rings which will be the signal for everyone to gather. Then each of the graduates will walk forward to receive their diploma. After the ceremony, there will be a picnic on the north side of the schoolhouse."

"Now, tell me about the wedding again, Mama."

Mama pressed her lips together in a tight smile. "Paulineee! Tomorrow morning we will all leave for Las Vegas... and the Justice of the Peace will pronounce your sister and Charles man and wife."

"And they will kiss like this"—Pauline puckered her lips way out while making a loud, smooching sound.

"Oh, Pauline, don't be silly. There is more to a marriage than smooching. It's sticking by each other through thick and thin. Even when you think you can't. Even when you think you don't like each other— much less love them. Look at your Daddy and me, and all we've have been through together. It wasn't always easy, and sometimes we were tempted to take it out on each other."

Pauline stopped her polishing—her mouth dropping wide open. "Mama, I can't believe what my ears are a hearin', you mean there was a time that you did not like my Daddy?"

"Pauline, it's 'hearing,' not 'hearin'. Oh, yes, Pauline, there were actually many times when I didn't like your Daddy. Now, I didn't say I didn't love him. Pauline, sometimes the love in a marriage can get buried down so deep, that a person can't see it, feel it, or hear it. There are times when you can even catch yourself forgetting love was even there..."

"Really, Mama, that's kinda scary."

"Pauline, it's not scary, it is just the part of life that God carries you through. I'll tell you one thing; it would be impossible to get through this life with any peace of mind without the Lord."

Pauline began gazing around the McCormick's kitchen. "Judas Priest, Mama, they must be rich! They have a water pump, a wood stove, and a real floor. I ain't never seen the likes of it."

"Pauline, your English."

"Sorry, Mama. I have never seen anything like this kitchen. Gosh, it just seems to take so many more words to say the same thing?"

"Where'd you get those eggs, Mama?"

"Mr. McCormick. Guess his wife told him about the festivities today. He kindly offered the ingredients for our cake."

"They have a chicken house?"

Pauline quickly put her polish rag down and jumped off of her stool heading toward the door. Mama grabbed her by the ear. "No, you don't, young lady! You will not be exploring an old dirty chicken house on an important day like today. You just sit right here and finish the task at hand.

"As I was saying, after June and Charles are married they will move into a little place, next to the railroad tracks, in downtown Mojave.

"Mama, you're calling Mojave a town? I could walk all of Main Street in five minutes."

"Pauline, it's the closest thing to a town you've ever seen. At least there is a gas station and a store. Of course, June and Charles will never go near that awful Whitey's Bar."

"After we save enough money for Daddy to drive to Long Beach, he will apply for work at the Naval Shipyard. You see Pauline; if we do go to war, workers will be needed to build and load ships and airplanes—not to mention keeping them in good shape. We'll be able to buy ourselves a home of our own.

"Oh, I'd best not carry on so; after all, only the Lord knows what the future holds. We can dream a little though, can't we, Pauline? Now let's get this cake over to the schoolhouse."

The ringing of the school bell signaled the start of the ceremony. The Lavaliere glistened in the sun as June, in her red high heels, walked down the earthen path between two rows of onlookers. The red silk tie framing the white collar on her polka dot blouse fluttered in the breeze. Her wobbly shoes shone in bright contrast against the various scarred and dusty pairs on both sides of her.

Pauline glanced over at Mama and Daddy just in time to see them wiping tears from their eyes. *Guess their dreams came true, and Mama's prayers were answered.*

That night Pauline laid out her sleeping bag so it touched June's. She reached over and put her arm around her sister.

"Pauline, why are you crowding me like this?"

"Don't think I am gonna be able to sleep. Mind keeps thinkin' 'bout tomorrow and the family headin' out for Las Vegas, then you and Charles taking off for Mojave. June, I just realized that this could be the last time we'll be sleeping side by side like this, and I'm gonna miss you."

"I will miss you, too, Pauline."

Tightly clasping their fingers together, June reminded Pauline that they wouldn't be very far away at all, and would most surely be back every weekend.

Chapter Twenty

July 21, 1939, was a blistering hot Vegas day. Immediately after Charles and June exchanged vows, the Sampleys departed. The newlywed couple took the lead in Charles' car. The remaining family followed behind in the Oakland. They barely made it to the state line before a familiar hissing emerged from under the hood of the Oakland.

The family coasted off the side of the road, steam shooting out from under the hood like a kettle on a stove. The Sampleys gathered in the shade of the two cars, parked bumper to bumper. After the radiator cooled and water was added, they continued on until a loud thump was heard from Charles' car. Everyone gasped as the car swerved and air spewed from the left rear tire. This time, with no available shade, Mama retrieved a quilt that she had used to cover the torn upholstery on the back seat of the car. Her hair blew erratically in the desert wind as she shouted orders. "Grab a corner of this blanket. It's up to us to provide the shade to keep the men from getting heat stroke."

It was dark when the clan reached the turn off to Uncle Amos' homestead and the The Golden Queen Mine to drop Delbert off for work the next morning. Both water bags were empty.

Charles and June had pushed ahead to Mojave, hoping to reach their rental near the tracks without their radiator running dry one last time.

After Charles and June departed for their own home, Pauline worried that Mama might miss the others... too much. She remembered how Mama had reacted when Delbert got the job at the Golden Queen Mine. Pauline found herself watching Mama, looking for symptoms—there were none. Charles kept his promise, and he, June, and Delbert drove back to the camp nearly every weekend.

During those weekend reunions Pauline, Mama, and Daddy huddled around June listening to her share stories of her week. She spoke of hobos jumping off the top of boxcars as trains slowed to pass through Mojave. At first, she was leery of opening her door to these homeless ones. Eventually, though, a sort of kinship evolved.

June boasted that she could detect the rumble of an approaching train from miles away. She said it wasn't long before she found herself anticipating the groaning whistle followed by a shy knock on the kitchen door. Throughout the week, she had begun, without thinking, to make up a plate.

Most days' drifters were June's only source of conversation—until Charles arrived home from the mine around dusk each evening.

On occasion, Delbert would join them for dinner. Afterward, the threesome would sit out front of their two-room house watching for a car to go by. June giggled, embarrassed, recalling times when they could surely be seen stretching their necks to peer around cactuses that threatened to obstruct their vision.

* * * * *

The money the Sampleys were tucking away for their future grew painfully slow. Charles contributed part of his pay to the fund, too.

Pauline seemed to have acquired a sudden motivation to get caught up in her studies. Maybe it was that nice Mrs. Jackson, or the fact that Mama was tutoring her again. Dale's grades were improving, too.

With the end of Pauline's school year in sight, Mama insisted that the family stay put until after graduation.

Pauline rolled her eyes, "Lord willin', and the creek don't rise."

Mama corrected her, "Pauline, it's 'willing' and 'doesn't rise.'"

"I swear Mama, this is the last time you will ever have to correct me. After all, I am just a hair away from becoming a high school graduate."

"Well, I certainly hope so, Pauline. Now, straighten those shoulders—you keep hunching over like that, and you'll stay that way forever."

* * * * *

June and Charles had arrived just after dusk. June hung her nicely pressed red skirt and red and white polka dot blouse on one loosely-flapping tie attached to the rolled up tent sides. Charles hung his sport coat on another. June cocked her head from side to side while brushing out a wrinkle or two.

The night was warm without the hint of a breeze. June was twisting wads of Pauline's damp hair around strips of rags and rolling them one at a time toward her scalp while tying each into a knot.

"How am I supposed to sleep in these things?"

"Pauline, tonight may not be the best night's sleep you will ever have. But, you are about to learn one last thing before you graduate tomorrow. It's not easy being beautiful. Chances are no one will sleep well tonight. Tomorrow is going to be one of the most important days of your life. Not only is it your graduation day, but just as we hoped—Daddy and Charles will take off after the picnic to scout out jobs at the Long Beach Naval Shipyard, and June will stay with us until we are all together again in Long Beach.

Daddy chimed in, "Yep, I hear tell jobs is a gettin' pretty plentiful with this here war a loomin'."

"Ouch. June, do you have to roll those rags so tight? You're going to scalp me!"

June ignored Pauline's plea, "Mama, what time is the graduation tomorrow?"

"Two o'clock, June. We should probably start getting ready right after lunch. Mrs. Jackson asked if we would come a little early to help set up."

"Mama, where do you keep the baking soda these days?" June asked. "I want to make up a paste for polishing the Lavaliere."

Pauline quickly came up with an old sock, handing it to June appreciatively. The girls hummed along peacefully as they recognized Daddy's version of the song "Old Black Joe" drifting in from somewhere nearby. June rubbed the Lavaliere in gentle circles just as Pauline had the year before.

"What are you going to read tonight, Mama?"

"Funny you would ask, Pauline; I was just thinking of asking June to pass me my Bible." Charles looked as if he didn't know what to do or where to be. His eyes shifted corner to corner of their enclosed space as if he was trapped. He appeared as if the Bible were a foreign book to him.

"Isaiah 35:7. *And the parched ground shall become a pool...*"

* * * * *

Pauline's face showed disbelief—*It's really me standing here on the threshold of the schoolhouse. Or should I pinch myself to make sure?* Instead, her hand reached for the Lavaliere to reaffirm her doubt. She sniffled as she noticed Mama wiping tears away and Daddy blowing his nose. *I never imagined I could really do it.*

Reaching out to receive her diploma she felt as if she were in a fog and all those in attendance were nothing but a blur.

After the family greeted everyone and the cake was cut, the Sampleys hurried over to the Oakland. Daddy and Charles had packed what they needed for the trip earlier in the day, as well as a tin of food to tide them over.

There was no sadness as Daddy drove away. Those left behind stood together—yet alone with their thoughts. Mama's voice was nearly inaudible, "Lot of hope in that car. A lot of hope." Motionless, they watched until the car faded out of sight.

* * * * *

Weeks passed with no word from Charles and Daddy. Delbert, being out at the Golden Queen, was isolated without a car to get to the camp. Uncle Amos had agreed to teach him to drive, and get him to Arvin Camp in time for their eventual move to Long Beach. Mama, June, Pauline and Dale had gotten on full-time at DiGiorgio's. Dale was able to take on a second job at a nearby Dairy Barn, that stressed that they hired only men.

By now, Mama had earned a reputation as a healer. People would come to their tent door day and night with everything from bronchitis to a backache to a splinter. She had never had any formal training, just remedies she picked up from her Mama and grandmother. Of course, she had years of experience at stitching, and had watched Daddy stitch many a forehead, finger, or toe. Pauline had grown accustomed to assisting Mama with her nursing. June left this task up to them, knowing how she usually grew faint at the sight of any kind of bodily fluids.

After a while, Pauline instinctively knew when Mama would need her to sterilize a needle, or make up a mustard pack, or a poultice of white bread soaked in milk. Mama refused anything but a hug for payment. Few had the means to pay, anyway. She left it at, "It's just the neighborly thing to do, Pauline."

Several days throughout the week folks brought food, making it nearly unnecessary for the family to be concerned about groceries. In their prayers they thanked God that they didn't have to use any of the emergency money Daddy had set aside for them.

Pauline's knowledge of car maintenance gave the whole family peace of mind. She was capable of changing a tire, checking hoses, brake pads, the battery and the oil. And if she hadn't had the opportunity to observe Daddy repairing something—she could usually figure it out on her own.

Mama and Pauline walked to the camp post office daily expecting a letter. The postal carrier eventually just shouted out the window, "No mail today, Sampleys!" as he saw them starting down the lane.

Finally, though, a letter did come. They sat close, hovering over it, June whimpering softly. Charles wrote:

Dear family,

I am sorry we couldn't write earlier. The first thing we did when Daddy and I arrived in Long Beach was to search for a boarding house near the Long Beach Naval Shipyard. We both agreed that would be the best place to start applying for a job. We secured a room to rent on the west side.

It was quite overwhelming when we reached the shipyard employment office. Yes, the lines were long, but, of course, we waited. My work at the mine seemed to interest them since they need many crane operators for loading and unloading the ships.

I was fearful when the outcome of Daddy's physical showed that he has a heart murmur and would be limited as to the jobs he could perform. Also, somewhat relieved that they didn't find anything more serious, after all he has been through with those dust storms. However, in the end, we are both full-time employees. The pay is excellent: $956 a year. We will have medical insurance, too.

Once we had that nailed down, we proceeded to focus on how to get everyone out here. We had not realized how hard the Depression had hit homeowners. We believe we are fortunate and here at the right time. During the Depression, so many lost their homes through foreclosures. It seems that the government is now attempting to turn things around.

The New Deal created the Federal Housing Administration that changed things a lot. They now have a 30-year mortgage and a reduced down payment.

Combining our wages, Daddy and I should bring in about $1,912 annually. If we get lucky and can buy a home for $3,500 and put 10 percent down, that's $350. We think we can do that! The bank should look favorably on the fact, too, that when we officially go to war, women should be able to get on at Douglas Aircraft. We will all need to share a house for a while, but I feel it is going to work. I really do.

As soon as we get the $350 in the bank, and the mortgage application is in the works, I will write to let you know. Meanwhile, we love you and the rest of the family. Be ready, we are anxious to see you.

Love,

Charles and Daddy.

P.S. It's heartbreaking, I know, but Daddy has decided that it will not be possible for Delbert to graduate from high school. He is nearly 21 and, between his CCC experience and his mining skills, the family needs the income he could provide. Sorry.

Mama, hands back in prayer position, clenched her top teeth tight over her lower lip as if trying to conceal a mix of emotions. "May your will be done, Lord."

Chapter Twenty-One

It was July 14, 1940. Ahead lay a strip of stark black asphalt separating rows of palm trees — shimmering in the afternoon sun. Mama sat upright in the front passenger seat next to Delbert, who was clutching the steering wheel. Pauline fingered a well-worn note. The camp boss had delivered it in person the day before. She read it aloud for what seemed like the one-hundredth time, *211 Lemon Street, Long Beach, California. White board house, painted red porch, red Bougainvillea on south side of porch, pine tree on north side of front walkway. P.S. Rose garden in back!*

Pauline shouted, "There they are, sitting on the porch waiting for us.

Mama's eyes smiled as she climbed the steps and cast herself onto Daddy's lap hugging him tightly. Charles and June seemed to melt into each others arms, dancing a slow dance. The others scurried past Mama and Daddy as they headed for the front of their new home. Pauline reached for the handle of the screen door when Daddy stopped her in mid-action, saying calmly, but firmly, "Let your Mama go first."

Embarrassed, the children stepped aside, falling in line behind her. Mama sucked in a deep breath as she slowly opened the screened door. She fixed herself on the threshold while taking it all in. The large bedroom that faced the pine tree. The side bedroom with a view of the neighbor's house. The narrow living room with tall sunny windows that overlooked the street. The dining room, with a bay window opposite the built-in china cupboards.

The motley group walked single file through the seemingly miniature kitchen, stopping now and then, while Mama demonstrated the faucet with running water, or opened the door to the icebox, or the oven.

The kitchen led the group into a laundry room that had obviously been added as an after-thought. Mama stood speechless, aghast with wonder as the family circled around a wringer washing machine.

"For Pete's sake, I saw Mrs. Yoder use one of these. You use this hose to fill the tub with hot water. You add your lye soap. You pull this long bar back, and agitation of the clothes begins. You run each piece of clothing through the wringer to squeeze the dirty water out. Then you repeat the same thing over again with clean rinse water. I'll bet there is even a clothesline out back for drying."

Mama appeared to be dreamily floating down the stairs into the backyard.

"Jack, would you look at this rosebud? And avocado trees, Jack. And back by the alley—a place for you to have a little workshop. The garage can be turned into two rooms, one for the boys and one for June and Charles. Pauline can have the second bedroom in the house with us."

Daddy gently placed his arm around Mama's waist, escorting

her back through the house to the floral sofa that was centered between two contrasting armchairs. The two sat facing the front screen door—Daddy's arm sliding up to rest on Mama's shoulder.

Delbert winked at Dale, "Come on, let's you and I bring stuff in."

* * * * *

The next morning, the boys swung the back door to the house open to the sound of water sloshing back and forth in the washing machine, and the sight of Mama drying her hands on her apron.

"Dale, you need to get cleaned up and put on your best clothes. Today, I will be registering you for school. Delbert, when we return, the car is all yours for job hunting."

"Thanks, Mama," Delbert replied. "I have my list of addresses that Charles made up for me. I just hope I can find my way around the big city."

Dale's mouth had dropped open. "Maaaa, you're going to need me around here. Plus, I could work on building a wall in the garage — making it more liveable."

"Nonsense. None of that takes precedence over your education."

"Precedence? What's that?"

"Exactly my point—we will leave here in forty-five minutes. Don't be late now."

* * * * *

Dale gawked openly as Mama pulled up in front of Wilson High School. He hung his head at the sound of the Oakland's tires screeching as they scrapped the curb.

Thick stone walls separated long sidewalks leading from one class to another, and then off toward the cafeteria. The students appeared older, or somehow more mature.

In the administration office, Mama sat next to Dale across from the principal, who held a clipboard that he periodically clipped and unclipped for no apparent reason.

"Ahem. Mrs. Sampley, what grade was Dale in when he last attended school?"

"Sir, he attended a one-room school house in Arvin Labor Camp near Mojave, California. I would say that Dale is probably a sophomore. I am a teacher, Sir, and I tutored my children, in addition to their schooling in the one-room schoolhouse they attended."

Mama attempted to ignore the sight in her peripheral vision—Dale staring out the window while Mr. Johnson was speaking. At the mention of testing, however, the sudden shuffling of Dale's feet caused Mama to give him a stern look. He cleared his throat.

Mama squared her shoulders and sat as tall as possible in her chair. Mr. Johnson, if you have a Bible, Dale can show you his level of reading."

"A Bible? Well, ah, ah... I do believe we will need to implement some placement tests. Have him here at nine tomorrow morning."

After dropping Dale off at school the next morning, Mama got down on her knees next to their bed and prayed: "Lord, take care of him. I know, Father, that you ask us to humble ourselves but, just this once Lord, I ask that you protect him from the trials and humiliation he may be facing on this day and maybe future days to come. Lead him to think clearly and remember all that he has learned. May he quickly catch up with his classmates, Lord.

I know that you know, that the circumstances he has walked through are due to no fault of his own. Amen."

* * * * *

Dale was relieved when he crossed the threshold into the room designated for testing. The room was filled with others who looked fearful and perplexed—like him. He was grateful for the sight of botched haircuts, pants that were too short and furrowed brows. A sudden awareness that he wasn't alone assured him that, *Yes, I can do this. Lord knows I've have been through worse.* He smiled at the others knowingly.

* * * * *

Mama hummed away cheerfully as she maneuvered gracefully in her well-equipped kitchen. She exhaled a deep breath while stretching across the table to place a platter of meatloaf and mashed potatoes before her family.

Dale struggled daily with the unfamiliarity of the big city school. A year after the first peacetime draft in the U.S. took place on October 16, 1940, Daddy signed for him to enlist along with his brother, Delbert.

Chapter Twenty-Two

Pauline clicked on the radio that overlapped a small bedside table next to them. Ever since the boys shipped out for military duty, June and Pauline had shared a bed again in the main house. Nightly conversations were kept low so as not to wake Mama and Daddy in their bedroom. The radio show host called herself 'Lonesome Gal.' The soothing voice of Rosemary Clooney singing, "You'll Never Know" flowed through the cloth-covered speaker. Pauline's mind drifted...

Was it chance that Daddy found a job in Long Beach? That Mama and Daddy found a home with so many unexpected luxuries?

Was it just plain luck that, with just a few changes, her brothers were able to bunk down in the garage, before Dale and Geraldine were married and the brothers went off to war?

Pauline's mind skipped back to that first day. She giggled recalling how the whole family had watched when the iceman came to a stop at the curb of their new home. With heavy steel tongs, he swung a block of ice off the back of his wood-floored truck. She remembered the whole family filing behind him one by one as he tromped through the living room into the kitchen. They watched while he placed a perfect-sized chunk into the small metal container in the center of the icebox.

Pauline grinned at the picture in her mind of the family peering into the bathroom as Mama tried the running water and the flush toilet. Her thoughts were interrupted by the sound of June's muffled sobbing.

She reached over to lightly touch her shoulder, "June, are you okay?"

"Yes, Pauline, I might as well tell you... Remember when I took the train to the east coast to see Charles when he was on leave? Well, one of those nights we talked long into the evening. Charles said he didn't know what the future would hold. He told me that he has never experienced the love he has felt since being part of our family. He wants our daughter to have a sister or brother so she can have the relationship that you and I have. Well, he got his wish. I'm pregnant!"

Pauline hugged June tightly.

"You are happy about the baby, aren't you, June?"

"Of course I am, Pauline. I'm only crying because I miss him so much. And because it is so dear that he wants our child to share the kind of love that you and I have. After all, how would you like to be an only child?"

"Wellll... there was a time... "

The two laughed, then lay side by side until quiet fell and the room was illuminated only by the streetlight glowing through the yellowed shade covering the window. It was then that the heavy breathing of the petite four-year-old sleeping in a crib at the foot of their bed lulled them to sleep.

* * * * *

Sitting at her dressing table—Pauline admired the boar-bristle brush that Mama and Daddy had given her for her nineteenth birthday. "Ummmm, my first real birthday gift ever."

She remembered Mama saying over and over again, "Boar bristle brushes put natural oil into the hair. You must brush your hair one-hundred strokes every night to keep it shiny." Pauline studied her image in the carved rose-framed mirror. Turning her head from side to side, she noticed that her hair was no longer red, but now a rich auburn color. She loved the feel of the sleek, soft curls sweeping across her shoulders.

The mirrored reflection of the wide-awake, petite, four-year-old interrupted Pauline's thoughts of herself. With tousled ringlets, the color of wheat, the girl sat perched on the edge of the chenille-covered bed—bare feet dangling. Pauline strained to hear the youngster humming an unfamiliar tune in near perfect rhythm to the swaying of her slender calves brushing against the soft white bedspread. It pleased her to see the child so content in her space.

Pauline reached for her perfume atomizer. Without a word, the child appeared at her side, with both wrists facing upward. How on earth could she have known? I barely made a sound. She was so engrossed in what she was doing. Pauline shook her head slowly and chuckled at the sight of the child standing next to her.

The ritual began—the hissing of the sweet smelling mist emerging after a gentle squeeze of the rubber bulb. The crisscrossing of Pauline's freckled wrists brushing against the child's pale, delicate skin, and the brief passing of the fragrance.

Pauline continued getting ready, not caring that the child ran her delicate fingers along the crevices of the crystal lamps perched on each side of her dressing table. She loved seeing the youngster's eyes sparkle as she gently clinked the dangles together.

Boosting herself back on the bed, the little one busied herself tugging and tucking the bedspread into a soft nest around her. Eventually, she sat with only her face, framed by a few tousled curls, poking out. It was then that she appeared satisfied. Pauline was unconcerned that the bed she had so carefully made, just a short time earlier, was now in disarray. Instead, she awaited the barrage of questions that were sure to come.

"Auntie, why are you getting all dressed up?"

"Well, baby girl, this is the first time our whole family will be together in a long time."

"Why?"

"The war, honey, World War Two.

"What's War Two, Auntie?"

"Well, a long time ago, before you were born, there were some countries way across the ocean that had bad leaders. One of those countries was Germany, and the leader's name was Adolph Hitler."

"Did Adol hit people?"

"I wish it was only hitting people, sweetie. You see, America and some other countries didn't like the bad things Adolph Hitler and others were doing to people, so they fought against the bad people, so good people like us would be safe and free.

"Uncle Dale was injured while he was in the Army. He was given a Bronze Star, a Silver Star and a Purple Heart. Not a heart like this heart of course"—Pauline patted her chest—"but one more like Grandma's brooch. When you see Uncle Dale in his uniform, you must look for those decorations.

"Today we're having a party to welcome your Daddy and Uncles home. They helped our country win the war. The soldiers won't have to be away fighting for us anymore."

The child gasped deeply. "Today is the day that Daddy is coming home? Does Mommy know?" A confused glaze crossed her face—followed by a long silence.

"Auntie, did Grandpa get a brooch?"

"No honey, Grandpa wasn't allowed to fight for our country— you see, when I was a young girl, people didn't take care of our good earth, and much of the soil turned to nothing but dust. When the wind blew, the dust turned the sky as black as night. Every breath we took was full of choking brown powder. Grandpa fought against the winds and the dust to keep us safe, and because of that, he could never breathe right again—his lungs"—Pauline held both hands across her chest. "We think that caused your Grandpa's heart murmur."

"During wartime, your Grandpa did what he could though. He was the neighborhood Air Raid Warden. He made sure all of the neighborhood lights were off when the air raid sirens sounded in a test drill so that if the enemy tried to attack us, we would be invisible at night. That's why we put black tape halfway down the car headlights too. And that's why Douglas Aircraft Company, just up the street, hid the entire top of the building and parking lot with a tent painted with pretend farmsteads and houses."

Wide-eyed, the child seemed to be searching the corners of the room with her thoughts spinning.

* * * * *

The two occupied themselves with their own thoughts until the girl spoke cheerfully, "What will I wear for the party, Auntie?"

"Ohhhhhh wait 'til you see!" Pauline opened the bottom drawer of her dresser revealing a child-size sailor outfit. "Your Daddy is going to be so surprised and so proud."

* * * * *

The two made their way toward the sound of Mama's butcher knife whacking fast and furious on a battered wooden cutting board. They entered the narrow kitchen to find her hunched over a pile of chopped celery, onions, and carrots. Pauline lifted the child up on the kitchen stool with the chipped red paint that had become the post from which she watched the preparations for chicken and noodles, but most often, more sparse meals

The child stared at her grandmother's quickly moving blade until it came to a halt. Pauline thought, *I know better than to offer to help Mama—she's waited a long time for this day, and it'll need to be her way.* So, they watched as she stood on her tiptoes scraping the minced vegetables into a large soup kettle that overlapped the burner on the stove. The savory aroma of a simmered stewing hen escaped from under a partially raised lid. *Oh, so this is why Mama has been saving those government food stamps. She bought a stewing hen.*

June scurried about the tiny kitchen behind Mama. She retrieved the needed items, and wiped down the counters, as Mama finished her peeling, slicing, and dicing. The youngster perched on her stool—took it all in, while waiting for her part that she knew was sure to come. Flour was sifted, and eggs added to Mama's yellow-striped mixing bowl. The stiff dough was rolled thin, covered with a dish towel and allowed to rest while the women poured themselves a cup of tea.

The women and June's daughter sipped tea and ate cookies while discussing the upcoming events. The child quietly listened while her grandmother made alphabet dots on a piece of paper for her to connect.

When it was time, Mama picked up where she left off with her short, muscular palms readying the dough before a heavy, wooden rolling pin flattened it thin. The child's eyes lit up at the sight.

"Grandma, can I do it?"

"When you are older honey. But, don't you worry, Grandma has a job for you. Patience is a virtue, you know."

The youngster watched with interest while her Grandma sliced the long rolls of dough that resembled jelly-rolls into thin pinwheels then gently tossed them into a mound of flour on the counter in front of her. It was time—the three women stood back beaming as a fine white puff of flour rose up, threatening to cling to the child's tight curls. Her dainty fingers separated each pinwheel into strips that she passed on to her Grandma who gently laid each one across a wobbly wooden drying rack.

* * * * *

Leaving the scene behind her, Pauline walked past the large Philco radio that sat catty-corner against the pale green dining room walls. The announcer's voice was familiar. "To date, industry has dismissed one in four working women. Twice as many quit voluntarily, choosing to return to domestic life after the upheaval of the war, opening jobs back up for our returning servicemen."

After the news broadcast, the snappy beat of Glen Miller's "In the Mood" filled the room. Pauline remembered the weekend before, dancing with the military men at the USO. They were always so polite and grateful.

On this day, the contagious beat of the song found her snapping her fingers and moving her hips to the beat of the music while dancing her way across the dining room and living room.

Sitting on the top step of the porch, Pauline tucked her skirt in around her—resting her elbows on her knees. Her eyes scanned the tree-lined, street dreaming of the sight of her brothers and Charles returning from military duty. The muffled sound of Vera Lynn singing "We'll Meet Again" caused Pauline to close her eyes and smile.

* * * * *

After dinner, Pauline sat on one end of the green floral sofa, soaking up each family member that had gathered in the small living room.

Mama looked as relaxed as a rag doll. Her shoulders drooped, but then her lips stretched into that familiar tight smile that pushed her cheeks up to the corners of her eyes as she leaned over to switch on a lamp.

Some sat close together on the ottoman, while others sat on a row of chairs carried in from the dining room. Mama's eyes glistened. Daddy insisted that Dale's wife, Geraldine, who was expecting any day, sit in the large overstuffed chair that had come to take on his shape. Dale, who was very thin from the malaria he suffered while overseas, scooted in next to her.

Once everyone was settled, Daddy spoke on a serious note. "So many memories—good and bad. I was so afraid we were going to lose Mama after Delbert left to work in the mine."

Charles, with his daughter on his lap, ran his fingers through June's hair. "I'll never forget the look on June's face when I was called to serve in the Navy."

June held out her palms in despair, "I felt torn, Charles. On one hand I knew serving our country was the right thing to do, but the thought of you leaving me and our little girl was overwhelming. I didn't want you to know about my selfish thoughts."

Their daughter wandered, seeming sidetracked, before stopping to search Dale's uniform for the Bronze and Silver Stars and the Purple Heart. Her small fingers stroked each one for quite awhile before she looked up into his eyes saying, "Auntie told me about these."

Delbert leaned forward with his forearms resting on his knees. "I'll never forget the day I shipped out. Women and children—strangers to each other, clustered together in the fog—most of them waving American flags. It was an unforgettable sight for sure."

June cleared her throat, "I remember clearly how I felt when Mama and Pauline started to work as riveters for Douglas Aircraft. I was so proud, but I felt I should have been helping too. I watched them get up early every morning and wrap their hair up in dish towel turbans to keep it from getting caught in the machinery. They walked to the bus stop on many a dark, foggy morning. They did their part back on the home front supporting the war effort."

Mama spoke up in defense of June's forlorn expression. "No one in the family doubts for a moment, June, that you wouldn't have been right alongside us, if you didn't have a child to take care of, and a second one on the way."

"You know what I'll never forget?" said Pauline, "Those posters in the lunch-room reading: *Good Work Sister, we never figured you could do a man-sized job!* and *America's Women Have Met The Test!* Guess that's just pure sinful pride coming out in me." Attempting to protect June's feelings, Mama snapped a quick look and a nod toward June, causing Pauline to quickly change the subject by asking Dale what stood out to him.

"Oh, not much, I guess. The biggest thing that came out of this for me is getting married to Geraldine, right here. He slipped his arm around her shoulder and gave her a kiss on the cheek.

Mama framed her face with her hands, "Oh my, all of the stepping stones it took to get us to where we are today!"

Meanwhile, the little one of the family restlessly meandered through the maze of laps, as if unable to choose the best place to be until her eyes rested on Mama's Treasure Chest. One finger delicately touched the edge of the box as if she suspected that touching it could be forbidden. Instantly, all family chatter ceased as unbeknownst to the child, everyone in their own mind slipped back to another time and place.

"What's in here, Mommy?"

"Oh, that's Grandma's Treasure Chest, sweetheart."

"What's a Treasure Chest?"

"It's a place where you keep things that are very dear to your heart."

"Can I see?"

Settling into the crevice of her Grandmother's lap, the latch was lifted and held open by two tarnished, gold chains. The child peeked inside of the threadbare velvet case. A sigh escaped her pursed lips when her Grandmother plucked the Lavaliere from off the top of the Bible.

"This, my dear, is the Lavaliere I wore when I married your grandfather. Your mother wore it when she graduated from high school and on her wedding day. Your Auntie wore it for her high school graduation, and you will wear it for your high school graduation."

The child fondled the ornate, gold backdrop that adorned the small ruby and dangling pearl. Then she leaned over the box questioning what was left inside.

"Oh, it's a book."

"Sweetheart, this isn't just any book, this is the Holy Bible. It's filled with true stories and tells us everything we ever need to know about right and wrong. It teaches us how to live our lives."

"Will you read me a story, Grandma?"

"I would love to read you a story, Jacklyn. I'll read you a Sampley favorite that our family has read countless times, across many miles. See how worn the pages are?"

In the midst of eyes shining with memories past, Mama began to read. "Psalm 23. *The Lord is my shepherd...*"